Cambridge Elements ☰

Elements in Campaigns and Elections
edited by
R. Michael Alvarez
California Institute of Technology
Emily Beaulieu Bacchus
University of Kentucky
Charles Stewart III
Massachusetts Institute of Technology

THE SOCIAL ORIGINS OF ELECTORAL PARTICIPATION IN EMERGING DEMOCRACIES

Danielle F. Jung
Emory University

James D. Long
University of Washington

CAMBRIDGE
UNIVERSITY PRESS

CAMBRIDGE
UNIVERSITY PRESS

Shaftesbury Road, Cambridge CB2 8EA, United Kingdom

One Liberty Plaza, 20th Floor, New York, NY 10006, USA

477 Williamstown Road, Port Melbourne, VIC 3207, Australia

314–321, 3rd Floor, Plot 3, Splendor Forum, Jasola District Centre, New Delhi – 110025, India

103 Penang Road, #05–06/07, Visioncrest Commercial, Singapore 238467

Cambridge University Press is part of Cambridge University Press & Assessment, a department of the University of Cambridge.

We share the University's mission to contribute to society through the pursuit of education, learning and research at the highest international levels of excellence.

www.cambridge.org
Information on this title: www.cambridge.org/9781009114264

DOI: 10.1017/9781009110280

First published 2023

A catalogue record for this publication is available from the British Library.

ISBN 978-1-009-11426-4 Paperback
ISSN 2633-0970 (online)
ISSN 2633-0962 (print)

Additional resources for this publication at www.cambridge.org/9781009114264.

The Social Origins of Electoral Participation in Emerging Democracies

Elements in Campaigns and Elections

DOI: 10.1017/9781009110280
First published online: August 2023

Danielle F. Jung
Emory University

James D. Long
University of Washington

Correspondence for authors: danielle.jung@emory.edu and jdlong@uw.edu

Abstract: Given the enormous challenges they face, why do so many citizens in developing countries routinely turn out to vote? This Element explores a new explanation grounded in the social origins of electoral participation in emerging democracies, where mobilization requires local collective action. This Element argues that, beyond incentives to express ethnic identity and vote-buying, perceptions of social sanctioning from community-based formal and informal actors galvanize many to vote who might otherwise stay home. Sanctioning is reinforced by the ability to monitor individual turnout given the open layout and centralized locations of polling stations and the use of electoral ink that identifies voters. This argument is tested using original survey and qualitative data from Africa and Afghanistan, contributing important insights on the nature of campaigns and elections in the promotion of state-building and service delivery, and the critical role voters play reducing fears of global democratic backsliding.

This Element also has a video abstract: Cambridge.org/Jung/Long_abstract

Keywords: Social sanctioning, developing countries, turnout, collective action, elections

ISBNs: 9781009114264 (PB), 9781009110280 (OC)
ISSNs: 2633-0970 (online), 2633-0962 (print)

Contents

Further online supplementary material for appendix can
be accessed at Cambridge.org/Jung/Long

1 The Stakes of Electoral Participation in Emerging Democracies

In many developing countries, unelected and unresponsive governments have often failed to provide the goods and services their citizens need to survive, let alone to thrive. People have turned to their communities – extended family and neighbors – to meet needs, from gathering funds to buy a child's school uniform to hitching a ride to a rural health clinic. Such informal ways of working together make survival less precarious for much of the global poor.

In recent decades, democracy's spread across developing regions has offered new pathways for people to improve their livelihoods. Democratic regimes formally allow citizens to demand public services beyond what they and their communities can provide for themselves, and to hold leaders accountable for the provision of those services. But to actualize democracy's potential and secure rewards from elected representatives, these communities – accustomed to self-reliance – must now mobilize their members to participate in elections.

Therein lies a dilemma: while residents individually and collectively benefit from living in a community with robust voter turnout, electoral participation takes time and effort, and those costs are borne individually. Any one person has incentives to free-ride on others' participation, even at the expense of the group's welfare. How citizens *and communities* overcome this predicament – central to democratic participation and consolidation – forms the focus of this Element.

Reconciling the costs and rewards from voting is far from straightforward, however. Motivations for and observed rates of turnout have long perplexed scholars. The time, energy, and opportunity costs associated with any single person voting are sufficiently large relative to the probability that their ballot proves decisive that a pure cost-benefit analysis would prompt few to turn out (Downs 1957; Riker and Ordeshook 1968). In transitioning democracies particularly, inchoate institutions, burdensome administrative procedures, challenges due to the electorate's sociodemographic profile, intimidation, and violence could all reasonably impose significant hurdles that deter participation.

Nevertheless, across democracies with different institutions and histories, citizens routinely show up on election day and often by wide margins compared to those who stay home. In fact, evidence shows that electoral participation is especially vigorous in new democracies, persists over time (Kostelka 2017; Kuenzi and Lambright 2007), and is often equivalent to or *higher* than in wealthier and more established democracies (Kasara and Suryanarayan 2015), where voting is easier. Figure 1 displays global turnout averages across legislative elections and demonstrates the vibrancy of participation in recent democratizers in Asia, Africa, Eastern Europe, and Latin America. Moreover, within

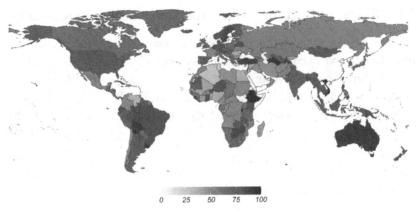

Figure 1 Average voter turnout (%) in most recent legislative election
Source: IDEA 2021

developing countries, research shows that groups of voters that might otherwise find it hard to organize, like the poor (Boulding and Holzner 2021) or rural inhabitants (Kuenzi and Lambright 2011), often participate at higher rates than those for whom voting is less demanding. What factors influence individuals' decision-making to overcome participation barriers, and how might their communities shape that decision?

1.1 Psychic and Material Explanations: Some Puzzles

While voting requires effort, resolving the puzzle of turnout would nonetheless seem straightforward: by showing that positive inducements eclipse any constraints, costs, and disincentives. Indeed, a rich scholarship from new democracies documents many such possibilities, focusing on a mix of psychic (intrinsic) and material (extrinsic) rewards. Psychically, individuals might experience joy by participating from an innate duty to democracy because of its newness (Bratton, Mattes, and Gyimah-Boadi 2005); likewise, they might experience intrinsic desire to vote to express their social identity (Dickson and Scheve 2006), an especially salient consideration in ethnically diverse countries with histories of sectarian conflict (Horowitz 1985). Materially, voters perhaps receive (or expect to receive) extrinsic incentives, such as gifts or cash, delivered by political agents in exchange for support (Kitschelt and Wilkerson 2007). Such vote-buying may prove especially effective in developing countries because much of the electorate remains poor; parties are believed to promise personalized benefits via patronage at the expense of broad programmatic policies (Chandra 2004).

These insights appropriately stress various positive influences on any potential voter. But under closer scrutiny, they fall short in fully explaining the impressive turnout observed across developing countries, and variation across voters within those countries. The logics underpinning these studies often point to radically different participation scenarios but lack clarity as to why.

Consider psychic benefits. That voters turn out to uphold democratic principles must be weighed against the possibility that citizens transitioning from dictatorship may not yet have significant knowledge of, or reasonable cause to signal support for, democracy. Expressions of duty also indicate levels of turnout will be highest in founding elections and then level-off as they become routine. Evidence supports this claim in older democracies (Franklin 2004) but does not appear to hold for newer ones (Kostelka 2017). The novelty of democracy could suggest either positive or negative turnout scenarios, depending on whether and in what ways duty affects the electorate. Psychic potential for expressive identity-based voting is similarly nettlesome. Although many developing countries are diverse and voters with strong social attachments are often the easiest to mobilize, citizens' reported feelings of in-group affinity are low. Only 16 percent of Afrobarometer respondents across more than a dozen countries expressed closeness to their ethnic group (Robinson 2014).

Or take material benefits. While vote-buying may counterbalance participation costs, the scale of payments candidates would need to make are likely unreasonably high to be feasible in poor countries, where weak parties, unconsolidated party systems, and a plethora of often disorganized coalitions mean that aspirants often do not have resources for extensive quid pro quo exchanges. In total, 82 percent of Round 5 Afrobarometer respondents said they had "never" received a gift from a candidate or party in the last election. Parties that succeed at evolving into hegemonic machines that dominate the electoral landscape (e.g., Mexico's Institutional Revolutionary Party and India's Congress Party) would appear to buck this trend by establishing expansive networks of village elites and party operatives who garner turnout through localized appeals to material incentives. But even where formal party structures attempt vote-buying by co-opting elites and leveraging informal networks, efforts are still highly targeted and do not often trickle down to the grassroots level (Stokes et al. 2013). Participation at the scale needed to win an election indicates recruitment and material drivers above and beyond what most candidates and parties, even machines, typically manage. Furthermore, contingent strategies based on material promises require politicians or their agents to monitor not merely *whether* a person voted but also *how*. Despite politicians' attempts to influence the process in other nefarious ways, survey evidence from Africa (Ferree and Long 2016) and Latin America (Nichter 2018) shows voters typically perceive their individual ballots to be secret.

In environments with unusually contentious elections, citizens confront an additional set of psychic and material considerations related to intimidation or realized election violence. Threats and attacks can arise from the actions of the government, opposition parties, and even insurgents. While violence should intuitively deter turnout, evidence shows prior exposure to it can *increase* political engagement and participation (Bauer et al. 2016), galvanizing disaffected citizens into meaningful action, like voting.

As a citizen weighs these costs and benefits, how do they decide whether to participate? Depending on how they calculate rewards, predictions on whether and why people vote point to different projections, and extant measures of psychic and material motives appear limited in explaining turnout likelihood. If those incentives do not tell the whole story, what does?

1.2 Social Sanctioning

We hope to resolve some of these puzzles by focusing on the *social* origins of electoral participation in emerging democracies. Most citizens do not make personal decisions about behavior in public life absent their social context, particularly when they lean on their communities for survival. We argue that social sanctioning, a combination of community-based pressure to vote and mechanisms to monitor turnout, alters the calculus of individual participation in ways not previously captured.

While voting is an individual action strictly speaking, we relate participation to the social problem of collective action. Voting represents a person's investment in *both* individual and collective goods (Popkin et al. 1976). People make this investment by showing up and casting ballots on election day, delegating to politicians the provision of those goods; once in office, leaders reward communities that supported them. Communities therefore signal enthusiasm via high turnout to make it more likely they obtain the collective benefits flowing from elected representatives – public services, club goods, and clientelism – compared to communities that participate at low rates. But locally targeted services help all in a community such that any resident has incentives to free-ride on others' participation. Because casting a ballot carries important implications for the citizen and their community, turnout is a cooperative dilemma that communities must overcome to support their collective interests.

If robust turnout indicates successful collective action, how have communities in transitioning democracies navigated coordinating behavior in new political waters? Answering requires examining whether and why individuals either free-ride (by staying home) or gain net positive benefits by turning out (participating) through "selective incentives" (Olson 1965). To identify the sources of these incentives, scholars have typically looked to how formal, institutionalized aspects of electoral competition map onto psychic and material rewards – for example, parties that mobilize voters with ethnic appeals or promises of bribes. But we suggest the introduction of competitive elections need not always rely exclusively on actions formally linking politicians and voters, especially where candidates are resource constrained, nor do they replace completely the many informal institutions and mechanisms that shape citizens' behavior. Instead, we propose to broaden the scope of selective incentives grounded in the practicalities of communal life by focusing on avoidance of negative punishments, which we term "social sanctioning," perceived by potential voters if they fail to engage in the community collective action of casting a ballot. Unpacking the social origins of selective incentives to prevent free-riding may resolve some perplexing aspects of participation.

Our conceptualization of social sanctioning has two broad components. First, communities in poor countries that regularly depend on self-sufficiency and mutual support have reasons to exert strong participatory expectations. While parties vary in their embeddedness in the political fabric, social networks and informal governance structures are often strong. As we demonstrate, there are many mechanisms that may reward and punish community members who conform (or not) to socially acceptable behavior that involves the community's welfare. Such norm enforcement follows actions of a variety of actors and institutions often overlooked in the study of campaigns and elections: household members, kinship groups, mutual aid organizations, and traditional, religious, or other thought leaders who often play a role legitimizing formal state institutions. The actions they adopt to compel norms of participation may work not only via positive inducements like vote-buying, but also by sanctioning through communal pressure – everything from a proverbial finger wag to denial of service at a local business or exclusion from government-provided resources.

Second, the electoral environment in emerging democracies facilitates these social dynamics of participation, if inadvertently. Administrative procedures aid communities in enforcing expectations to vote by providing opportunity and capacity to monitor turnout. Whether in cities or villages, communities are clustered tightly around schools, houses of worship, and market centers that serve practical purposes and provide social meaning to people's lives. On election day, such locations also serve as polling precincts. Voting often requires long, public queuing, and area residents can – and do – observe who votes, even if individual ballot choice is secret. Moreover, voters' fingers are often marked with ink. While inking has been employed to prevent fraudulent double-voting, this easy verification also facilitates monitoring efforts on election day and for days after.

Asserting strong expectations to vote in combination with the ability to monitor participation allows communities to solve the cooperation problem and achieve higher turnout by creating the perception that people should vote, and that those who do not will face sanctioning. Candidates and party agents certainly remain important for both mobilization and monitoring, but they improve these efforts by coordinating with other local, often informal, actors. And individuals certainly confront the possibility of other psychic and material incentives, but communities also apply a new type of incentive through social sanctioning to voters who might otherwise stay home.

By focusing on the social origins influencing individual behavior, we explore an extension of our theory specifically applied to countries suffering significant violent conflict: whether variation in social capital influences the degree of social sanctioning necessary to induce cooperation. Social capital, determined by community levels of trust and perceptions of reciprocity, shapes the degree to which coordination on community action – like voting – strengthens or attenuates. But perpetual fighting and political instability, characterizing the most vulnerable democracies, plausibly improves or degrades those levels of trust. Leveraging data from an active conflict setting, we postulate that where individuals express more trust in their neighbors, communities need not provide as many inducements to generate cooperative behavior compared to areas where trust is weaker. That is, more trusting individuals are more likely to vote in the absence of social pressure, whereas less trusting individuals require more pressure. In this way, violence and instability may play roles affecting participation in fragile democracies less as a result of their direct effect on voters' behavior, and more from how trust mediates social sanctioning and cooperation in communities that experience ongoing conflict.

1.3 Testing the Argument

We explore electoral participation in contemporary emerging democracies. Decolonization in Africa and Asia, cycles of dictatorship and democratization in Latin America and Southern Europe, the fall of the Soviet Union, and the end of the Cold War all catalyzed a so-called "third wave" of democratization across much of the developing world by the late twentieth century (Huntington 1993). This wave has continued into the twenty-first century due to factors such as violent regime change from foreign intervention or state collapse, the Arab Spring revolutions in the broader Middle East, and internationally supported state-building in weak states. Across these diverse settings, turnout certainly varies given the enormous challenges voters face, but it nonetheless persists. While our theoretical intuition reflects features that many developing countries share, cases from third-wave African democracies (Ghana, Kenya, and Uganda) and a fragile state (Afghanistan) are especially pertinent to explaining the emergence of electoral participation and its social origins.

First, these countries broadly share many institutional and economic features, as well as social dynamics, that differentiate them from older, industrialized democracies. In the former, lacking sustained economic development, residents of many communities require public services to meet basic survival needs; the transition to democracy plausibly provides new channels. Voters frequently select leaders on the basis of expected distributive action, particularly with respect to local public goods. But because politicians face tight budgets, they often confront stark trade-offs regarding where to apply such spending to increase the likelihood of electoral victory. Unlike consolidated democracies or countries with class-based mobilization, voters in many third-wave democracies cannot align themselves with candidates or parties based on long histories of programmatic performance or ideological orientations; similarly, there are limitations to individualized rewards politicians can credibly deliver. This does not make programmatic actions impossible nor suggest patronage is altogether absent in new democracies, but it does indicate that they are not the only material considerations for voters – the extent and quality of local services also matter and form a basis on which to pick and judge leaders.

Second, in selecting recent democratizers that confront a variety of institutional weaknesses, our cases provide rich portrayals of local environments through which social sanctioning could operate. These include identifying the breadth and depth of an array of actors and mechanisms, which often predate democratic transitions, that support community-based collective action to assist citizens' well-being. The density of social networks suggests capacity – latent or extant – that could be plausibly put in service of electoral aims. Considering the prevailing belief that the salience of ethnicity and pervasiveness of vote-buying largely determine electoral behavior in third-wave countries, ours are particularly suitable and "hard test" contexts to evaluate our predictions alongside alternatives. We also chose cases with prior sporadic histories or expectations of voter intimidation and/or election violence, and a fragile state where election attacks are frequent, the regime unstable, and there is ongoing conflict that may have eroded social capital. To further underscore participation's social origins, the countries share plurality electoral rules but vary in party systems, since the number and types of parties affects turnout, at least to a degree, given the organizational strategies of formal political actors. However as we explain, our aim is not to leverage party system variation but rather to show that the social drivers of turnout can be found across institutional settings.

Last, our theory applies well in third-wave democracies because of how they administer elections, informed by our experiences observing them (including in our four country cases). Voting is a public act organized around area focal points that carry important political and social meaning in citizens' lives. Beyond the hassle of long queues and communal nature of voting, finger inking allows turnout verification.[1] Compared to industrialized democracies, community members can more easily and consistently monitor participation.

After unpacking our theoretical components in Section 2, we examine their empirical implications in Ghana, Kenya, and Uganda in Section 3 . We combine new quantitative survey data with other administrative, qualitative, survey, and ethnographic data to assess the plausibility and breadth of the role of social sanctioning alongside expressive ethnic voting, vote-buying, and violence across three party systems. Section 4 presents Afghanistan, whose democracy had been dangerous, hard-fought, and fledgling over the past two decades, before evaporating after the Taliban's takeover in 2021. Afghanistan represents perhaps the hardest assessment of electoral participation in a weak and conflict-prone country of the type that is subject to twenty-first century state-building. Section 4 includes improvements to survey-based empirical measures from Section 3; Afghanistan also permitted an examination of legislative elections with no party system and investigation into how trust and social capital condition the effects of social sanctioning.

Section 5 generalizes and relates our findings to scholarship and policy on political behavior, campaigns, and elections in developing democracies, where representative institutions and electoral participation are newer, less studied, and voting costlier, relative to established democracies. It also expands on the role that the social origins of participation can play in conversations about growing concerns regarding global democratic backsliding.

2 A Theory of Social Sanctioning

2.1 Participation as a Problem of Collective Action

A pure cost–benefit analysis would suggest few reasons to vote, yet many people do, including and especially in emerging democracies. Scholars have focused on an individual's expected utility calculation to weigh how variation in psychic and material factors change participation propensity.[2] But such approaches may point

---

[1] At least ninety countries mark voters with ink (Darnolf et al. 2020). Inking is particularly common in Africa, South/Southeast Asia, and the Middle East/North Africa, but less so in Latin America (Ferree et al. 2020), although some countries like Bolivia and Brazil allow checks of individual turnout from administrative records.

[2] Adopting Riker and Ordeshook's (1968) classic model of turnout calculus, psychic and material motivations can be modeled as parameters entering an individual's utility function, with a positive

to low or high turnout, or a mix, depending on various individual and contextual factors. On balance, what ultimately pushes individuals to the polls?

To answer, we look at citizens who might consider staying home due to costs they may incur (e.g., time to queue, potential for violence). But departing from studies that focus on the decision to participate as solely arising from shifts in an *individual's* utility resulting from changes to psychic or material payoffs, we locate our theory within an Olsonian collective action framework to examine participation's *social* origins. Specifically, we are interested in the role that a previously overlooked type of selective incentives – social sanctions imposed by communities – play in generating turnout.

Our theory assumes that a citizen's vote constitutes a personal investment in individual and collective goods. Communities better able to participate through voting are more likely to benefit from elected representatives. "Community" refers to the locale in which a person lives and the spatial designation for clustered voters with shared interests, including immediate and extended families and other area residents. Who and what constitute these environments is highly contextual and undoubtedly varying, even within countries; but such clustering often corresponds to how voters are distributed near polling centers – like schools, market centers, and houses of worship – in both cities and villages. These focal points provide both practical and social meaning to people's everyday lives; on election day, they serve as polling centers. Because lawmakers legislate and distribute goods to locales (e.g., constituencies, districts) as rewards that will benefit some at the expense of others, turnout signals grassroots enthusiasm; without representation, a community receives little government largesse. Turnout therefore requires collective action.

Like all collective action problems, members enjoy shared goods whether they pay the personal cost to participate, creating incentives to free-ride on the contributions of others. Communities' ability to impose negative incentives (social sanctions) to prevent free-riding is critical; as we demonstrate, accounting for individual- and community-level benefits can shift an individual's utility and therefore behavior, but also the behavior of others.[3] Because participation

---

expectation of voting expressed as the inequality $pB+D>C$, where p is the probability a voter's ballot is decisive, B is the utility they receive given candidates' positions or characteristics, D is the intrinsic "duty" they feel toward democracy, and C is their cost of voting. Given a low value of p and constant B, an individual is likely to vote when their psychic duty outweighs costs, $D>C$. Gerber, Green and Larimer (2008) extend this logic by further dividing D's utility into both intrinsic (psychic, DI) and extrinsic (material, DE) elements, where $D=U(DI, DE)$ and the value of D (and likelihood of voting) grows with increases from both (or either) DI or DE – similar to reducing the magnitude of C (reflecting that some costs are offset by rewards).

[3] Distinguishing between individual and community is important because modeling voting as a problem of individuals' utility maximization focuses on parameters that increase likelihood of turnout – like C, D, DI, or DE – that are act and not outcome contingent: individuals would

operates at the individual *and* community levels, we reference both as occurring at a "local" level to indicate *where* and *why* we believe community pressure will most pertain, highlighting socially rooted drivers of turnout.

These dynamics are strongest at a localized, community level for several reasons. Our intuition follows Olson (1965), who argues smaller groups more easily overcome free-riding, not due to their size per se but their ability to monitor. As group size grows, monitoring becomes more difficult; as it declines, easier. Moreover, communities in emerging democracies are better positioned to overcome Olsonian scale issues for reasons bounding our theory: they are more accustomed to depending on one another and can more easily observe turnout. We do not suggest that cooperation arises *exclusively* from community interests and organizational capacity – how formal actors try to leverage access to shape behavior remains relevant, and political parties succeed when facilitating electoral participation among larger groups. However, even where parties or other organizing bodies are strong, but especially where they are weak, there are also ways to exert pressure as a function of how those parties work with and within communities, and what communities and their leaders do on their own.

How and why these dynamics play out locally also reflects the logic of political survival in developing democracies. Suppose a politician can legislate and deliver at one, two, or all three of three levels: programmatic public goods to the entire country, targeted club goods (local public goods) to certain districts or areas within those districts, and private goods to specific individuals. These levels differ in excludability: a pure public good is enjoyed by all; club goods are nonexcludable in the locations where they operate (like a village's well) but are effectively excludable to those who reside outside that area; and private goods are enjoyed by the individual and excludable to everyone else, even other area residents.

The impact of the distribution of goods within and across these levels matters because it shapes strategies that attempt to influence voters based on how they perceive politicians' performance. A leader pursuing national-level policies believes voters will condition support partly on programmatic performance, as well as on some community effect to the distributive action (whether indirectly or directly) from policies or spending that trickles down (or not) to the local level. By design or happenstance, different communities will enjoy different levels and quality of these benefits. For club goods – which members of a community enjoy but do not share with those from the outside and can be targeted by (both national and local) politicians in the form of clientelism or pork-barrel spending – distribution need only have some local effect, echoing

---

receive payoffs for voting regardless of the outcome and whether anyone else voted. In contrast, our model asserts that part of an individual's decision-making is formed by their expectations of others' behavior.

the push and pull factors that are aspects of politicians' distributive behavior in return for electoral backing. At either the national or district level, from the trickle-down effects of programmatic benefits or the positive returns from club goods, localized support from a community matters to national and local politicians' electoral chances.

Importantly for our theory, our account contrasts with two other common perspectives on politicians' actions regarding their political survival. The first is found in wealthier and more consolidated democracies, where politicians typically follow redistributive patterns that explicitly pursue programmatic benefits over clientelism and patronage, all else equal. Because advanced welfare states already effectively raise incomes, tax, and enact policies benefiting the median voter (both nationally and within a district) given the actions of politicians who benefit/suffer from established party reputations (typically along a left–right dimension), directing goods to some communities and not others, or some individuals and not others, runs the risk of hurting electoral chances. Forms of pork, vote-buying, and patronage might also be both illegal and effectively prosecuted, or otherwise inefficient at swaying the median voter. But in developing countries, clientelism supposedly matters precisely because of sensitivity to local conditions due to the government's poor economic progress nationwide; the government's inability to finance programmatic policies, or enjoy established reputations for doing so, given the recency of democratic transition; the prevalence of political favoritism; and budget limitations with weak enforcement that encourage pork.

The second viewpoint is reflected in many prevailing views of the role of patronage in developing democracies. This scholarship often conflates district-level clientelism with individually targeted incentives, but it is worth distinguishing them in our framework because they potentially operate on voters in different ways and for different reasons. While vote-buying and patronage might offset an individual's cost of voting, it would do nothing for the community; whereas clientelism is enjoyed by the community regardless of whether the individual participates – in the absence of other inducements, their participation would result only in costs (not benefits) to them, inspiring few to vote.

Certainly, clientelism need not preclude programmatic policies nor patronage in a politicians' distributional logic entirely; politicians may pursue a multi-pronged strategy. Furthermore, communities that fail to mobilize probably do not lack services *entirely*. However, we focus on who enjoys the good and at what level, particularly when it is localized and therefore excludable, because voting for a representative is an important means to avoid marginalization from the budget, pork, and discretionary government policy-making that matter locally. All else equal, communities unable to cooperate would lack representation relative to those who do, and therefore communities have incentives to vote in order to maximize local benefits via national politicians and those within their districts.

2.2 Theoretical Framework

2.2.1 Individual Actions and Community Outcomes

Our theoretical framework and predictions examine conditions under which individual and population features increase participation. Specifying strategies and payoffs at the individual and community levels allows us to explore how communities overcome collective action problems to increase turnout among citizens who understand its likely costs. Empirical implications (Section 2.3.3) are derived from an agent-based model (ABM), detailed in Appendix E[4]; using nontechnical language here, we describe our logic regarding sources, levels, and motivations for turnout.

Aggregate participation is analogous to patterns of cooperation within a population faced with prisoner's dilemma–ordered payoffs. For simplicity, suppose a community in a new democracy has two individual citizens who are potential voters, V_1 and V_2, depicted in Table 1. First assume neither participates but instead defects with the action "stay home" (bottom-right). The payoffs at the *community* level are negative: since neither bothered to vote to delegate the provision of services to the government, the government in response has little incentive to provide those services. Payoffs at the *individual* level if both "stay home" are mixed: neither gain psychic[5] or material benefits, both potentially suffer social sanctioning (we explain social sanctioning as a basket of negative selective incentives in Section 2.3), yet neither incurs costs such as losing time and wages, or possibly experiencing violence.[6] To capture contexts with violent election days, we term this payoff "violence," but this is analogous to real or anticipated harmful effects of participation short of actual violence (like intimidation).[7]

---

[4] ABMs are useful theoretical tools to explore how levels of cooperation vary based on the actions of individuals and how those decisions interact with others' to understand population-level outcomes (a particular concern in games of repeated play, see Jung and Lake (2011a), Jung (2012), and Jung and Lake (2011b)).

[5] Expressive voting would occur by increasing the benefits a voter feels from D, such that $D>C$; or be modeled as DI.

[6] This could take place by either reducing the magnitude of C, or – if large enough – by a net positive gain rather than a negative cost if the magnitude of material incentives exceeds the costs; or be modeled as DE.

[7] Violence could affect voters directly via D or C, or indirectly via a psychic reaction through DI if memories of previous violence cause anger (motivating participation) or fear (demotivating participation). We remain agnostic about the precise mechanism, acknowledging that violence may manifest along different pathways for different voters.

Table 1 Electoral participation as a collective action problem

		Voter 2	
		Participate	*Stay Home*
Voter 1	*Participate*	Community outcome **Higher investment** *Individual outcomes* V_1 & V_2: **Benefits**: Psychological benefits, potential social benefits, material benefits, access community benefits **Costs**: A day's wage, risk of violence	Community outcome **Middling investment** *Individual outcomes* V_1: **Benefits**: Access community benefits, psychological benefits, material benefits **Costs**: A day's wage, risk of violence V_2: **Benefits**: Access community benefits, keep day's wages, no risk of violence **Costs**: No psychological or material benefits, potential social sanctioning
	Stay Home	Community outcome **Middling investment** *Individual outcomes* V_1: **Benefits**: Access community benefits, keep day's wages, no risk of violence **Costs**: No psychological or material benefits, potential social sanctioning V_2: **Benefits**: Access community benefits, psychological benefits, material benefits **Costs**: A day's wage, risk of violence	Community outcome **No investment** *Individual outcomes* V_1 & V_2: **Benefits**: No lost work or time, no violence **Costs**: No psychological or material benefits potential social sanctioning, no community benefits

A second scenario assumes V_1 and V_2 both cooperate and "participate" (upper-left). Community payoffs are positive, including higher investment in the likelihood of gaining government services. Individually, both receive positive psychic rewards, may receive private excludable material payoffs, and avoid negative social sanctioning – but they pay costs in terms of time/ wages and potentially violence. (The individual-level outcomes might not be shared equally between V_1 and V_2, but both nonetheless face costs with "participate".)

In a third and fourth scenario, the upper-right and lower-left cells indicate the result if either V_1 or V_2 cooperates ("participate") while the other does not ("stay home"). Even if one citizen takes the "sucker's" payoff and votes while another free-rides and does not, turnout is lower overall. At the community level, there is middling investment in collective goods – a lower probability that leaders will look favorably on that community compared to when both turnout and invest-ment is higher. For communities in our third and fourth scenarios, more moderate turnout decreases the likelihood that they elect a local candidate relative to higher turnout locales that can communicate the community's needs to politicians – that is, noncooperative outcomes signal some enthusiasm to government but at a lower rate. Individually, the person taking the sucker's payoff gains psychic and material rewards for voting, avoids social sanctioning, but pays costs and risks violence; the citizen who stays home does not receive additional benefits, potentially experiences social sanctioning, but does not pay costs or risk violence.

Table 1 highlights numerous factors accounting for turnout and subsequent payoffs for communities and individuals based on individuals' strategies and the success (or not) for cooperative behavior. Certainly, citizens receive and incur individual costs and rewards for voting in ways reflecting intrinsic and extrinsic motivations. However, people's motivations include not just what they expect to gain individually but also how electoral outcomes affect provision of goods to their area and the likely behavior of others. Since spoils accrue to local residents, citizens do best if they coordinate to vote, fielding a candidate to bring them benefits. Voting is a political action but derives in part from social roots.

Before proceeding with our discussion of social sanctioning, we offer a few clarifications. Our theory's key intuition is that putting a candidate over a winning threshold into government matters most. However, if candi-dates or communities see incentives to generate over-sized victories, the salience of community payoffs likely increases. Such dynamics occur in dominant party systems where parties generate wide vote margins to achieve constitutional super-majorities (e.g., South Africa's African National Congress) or to signal unrivaled political dominance (e.g., Mexico's Institutional Revolutionary Party).[8]

Additionally, in our framework electoral participation is both act *and* out-come contingent. Our theoretical interest is driven by the puzzle inherent in collective action: when benefits are shared, why do citizens pay the individual costs of participation even if their contribution is unlikely to affect the outcome? Solving this tension requires narrowly explaining an act-contingent behavior. But the assumption driving our analogy also implies citizens care about the actual outcome and whether the winning candidates distribute goods to reflect participators' preferences. We believe this is true for several reasons.

---

[8] Consistent with our theory, Rosenzweig (2019) shows that communities may sanction abstaining voters even in strictly authoritarian settings due to their expectation that high turnout induces greater access to public goods.

First, citizens in transitioning democracies frequently condition electoral behavior on politicians' performance, despite choosing between parties/candidates that do not develop policy platforms along clear ideological or class lines, and who frequently do not enjoy long-established reputations from having served in elected office over many election cycles (Hoffman and Long 2013). Even in contexts where governments lack distributional capacity, such as fragile democracies, citizens still demonstrate regime compliance in ways expressing demands for services (Berman et al. 2019). In Haiti, despite state collapse, multiple nonstate providers (including gangs), and high approval rates for vigilante justice, citizens still favor the government to provide law and order (Jung and Cohen 2020). Sensitivity to an elected government's actions suggests connections between election outcomes in the second instance as influencing the probability of participating in the first instance, and in addition to any intrinsic feelings from voting or direct quid pro quo exchanges.

Second, although voters might lack deeply rooted relationships with politicians expressed through formal party memberships, citizens and leaders are still frequently tied through multilayered personal, familial, and social connections. As a result, winning candidates often cultivate a "personal vote" and garner blocs of clustered votes in their communities relying on strong support from extended family members, neighbors, and kinship groups. Voters often know by sight or association candidates formidable enough to win office and understand that greater community turnout increases distribution to them relative to lower turnout. Even if the same locale yields multiple contenders (including under hegemonic party systems where multiple individuals compete for one nomination), community members still must cooperate to turn out the community, and the strongest candidates are those best known to the areas they (intend to) serve.

2.3 Social Sanctioning

How do communities mobilize individuals to achieve collective action and a cooperative equilibrium (both V_1 and V_2 participating, Table 1 upper-left)? As V_1 and V_2 weigh various incentives and costs, each also wants to avoid the penalty of what we term "social sanctioning," which has two core components that influence behavior: strong expectations and pressure to participate on the part of community members, and the ability of the community and other actors to monitor individual turnout.

2.3.1 Community Expectations and Pressure

The structure of local society in developing countries offers many pathways through which communities can express strong expectations to vote or are perceived as such. Fear of being – or the fear of exposure as – a violator of norms induces people to behave in ways they might otherwise not: participating when they may rather stay home. Perceptions of sanctioning arise because communities convey the importance of their members to participate and pressure them accordingly.

Citizens in poor countries often lack basic services and suffer perilous security and economic conditions. The practices and institutions supporting self-help and communal solidarity emerge and persist precisely where people face an "existential dilemma" of economic uncertainty (Scott 1977); they therefore turn to their extended family, neighbors, other community members, and local nonstate actors, for assistance. At a personal level, this could involve borrowing money from a relative to pay school fees; from the community, it could involve mutual assistance or management of locally shared resources through successful collective action (Ostrom 1990). Principles and standards of reciprocity help set expectations of redistributive action, physical security, and economic well-being for people in developing contexts (Platteau 1991).

With the advent of democracy, formal government institutions possibly provide a new avenue to improve community welfare via government-provided distributional mechanisms – but only if members mobilize to the polls. Communities therefore have reasons to expect their members to vote to improve community welfare and to sanction those who do not.

The potency of this custom is revealed by empirical evidence underscoring the belief among large majorities in recent democratizers that being a "good citizen" is tightly linked to voting. Out of the Round 6 Afrobarometer respondents, 80 percent replied that voting is something a good citizen "always" does, while only 18 percent replied "if they so choose." Participation provides as means of strengthening social bonds and showing that one is a member in good standing. As expressed by a woman in Namibia, "Voting allowed [her] to experience herself as a member of a community of equals whose voices count . . . . Voting, in short, was a fundamentally social experience . . . . It presented an occasion to meet and created a moment of *communitas* that reaffirmed the village's political sphere" (Dobler 2019: 18).

While political parties vary in their degree of institutionalization or embeddedness in the political fabric of transitioning societies, social networks are often strong. Communities have many formal and informal mechanisms and actors to help enforce cooperative norms. We do not make, nor does our theory require, strong claims regarding the precise form or magnitude of the sanction, meaning the rate at which sticks are rendered, or specifically by whom – this no doubt varies by sanctioner/sanctionee, and by local and national context. It also need not be a coordinated effort by the entire community but could occur between individuals working on the community's behalf. In Sections 3 and 4, we discuss similarities and differences influencing perceptions of social sanctioning in our cases. Here, we briefly review how preexisting social dynamics in developing countries generally can be brought to bear to help communities gain the most from democratization.

One way communities convey expectations to vote is by leveraging in-group pressure, where violating conventions leads to ostracization and opprobrium that potentially entails punishment (Greif 1993). Neighbors, other community members, or local businesses might shun a violator (e.g., by denying service) with costs varying in terms of whether they are carrots or sticks, and in severity. Sanctions could manifest as exclusion from government-provided goods managed at the local level, like health facilities, or common-pool resources, like land for grazing. "Sanctioning" is a useful shorthand but does not require administration of extensive punishments. Although the effect is likely strongest with a credible threat, expectations alone may also be quite powerful – that is, pressure need not be overt or even realized, the *perception* of these prospects may have an effect (whether correctly or incorrectly assessed). Because social sanctions may be administered by a wide variety and number of community members and take various forms, combined with the diffusion of this task over the community, its administration is relatively cheap and its potency in driving participation is likely to be strong. This falls in contrast to most forms of patronage, which distribute *positive* (and expensive) selective incentives, by and for a select group. That is, even small shifts in perception or application of social sanctioning at the individual level can reinforce beliefs and trigger a community-wide "tipping point," inducing perhaps unexpectedly widespread turnout overall in ways vote-buying cannot.

Other social foci create and reinforce pressure, which exist separate and apart from elections but nonetheless prove useful reminding community members of the importance of participation. Familial and kinship ties are one source because voting is often literally and metaphorically a "family affair." Members of households travel and cast ballots together, as in Namibia, where "Everybody in a household knew when and where the other household members cast their vote. Older people tried to make sure their dependents were seen taking part in the elections" (Dobler 2019: 18). In India, "[n]ot to vote would be akin to not celebrating your child's wedding – conceptually possible, but so curmudgeonly, eccentric and anti-social that only a tiny minority would want or dare not to do it" (Banerjee 2007: 1558–9).

Mutual aid organizations coordinate grassroots action toward a variety of purposes aimed at improving communal welfare and the "economic 'insurance' for their members" (Ames 1959: 224), including electoral mobilization. The Senegalese relate local economic conditions to voting, which provides a means "to build relationships with electoral patrons and to obtain material rewards from them, as well as occasions to reinforce ties of solidarity that may be called upon in times of crisis" (Schaffer 2003: 80); as such, "[w]omen's *groupements* form one of the most powerful voting blocs in Senegal. Highly organized, these groups meet frequently and regularly, devise political strategy, and wield great power and influence over politicians and government actors" (Kah et al. 2005: 143).

Norm enforcement also follows the actions of local notables who often play a role in promoting and facilitating collective action and endorsing state institutions – thought leaders, opinion shapers, and political mobilizers. Baldwin (2016) notes that since the introduction of multiparty politics in Zambia, traditional chiefs have served as intermediaries between political parties and residents at the grassroots level. Given levels of religiosity in much of the Global South, religious leaders serve as important mediators of political messaging (Dreier et al. 2020), often calling upon voters to turn out to support democracy and for politicians to repudiate violence. Church organizations conduct voter education and outreach, and members often vote together and serve as accredited observers.

Because party strength varies widely in developing countries, evidence underscores the importance of candidates relying on informal vote "brokers," or local agents (often self-declared) acting as go-betweens for leaders and community members during election periods. Brokers are valuable because they communicate citizen demands of government to politicians (Gottlieb and Larreguy 2020) and coordinate residents' participation through a mixture of positive and negative inducements (Mares and Young 2016; Stokes et al. 2013). Across our cases, we show how brokers are an asset for politicians by providing "eyes and ears" on the ground during campaigns, often exploiting connections with others viewed as local authorities; like in Paraguay, where aspirants identify community leaders to mobilize voters by activating sentiments of reciprocity between the electorate and politicians (Finan and Schechter 2012). Brokers also assist with monitoring turnout, as we discuss next.

2.3.2 Community Monitoring

The electoral environment in emerging democracies facilitates the social dynamics of participation and in ways unique from many industrialized democracies. Administrative procedures aid cooperative behavior, if inadvertently, given features of the balloting process. While vote *choice* is usually private, guaranteed by a secret ballot, *turnout* choice is frequently visible. To apply pressure among possibly fickle voters, community members can create the perception of observing individual behavior among themselves and by other actors working for the community's interests. Whether realized or not, the capacity to observe is an important component of how social sanctioning drives turnout.

In cities and villages, communities are physically clustered around village focal points – schools, community and market centers, houses of worship – that serve everyday purposes infused with practical and collective meaning, and function as polling precincts. Polling centers typically host a few hundred to a few thousand voters that directly reside in the surrounding area. Voting is often on a public holiday when schools, offices, and businesses are otherwise closed amid a celebratory mood. It is necessary to travel and wait on public roads and access points into polling locations, and most stations involve visible queuing for an extended period (as demonstrated by our observation in urban, Figure A.1, and rural, Figure A.2, Ghana). Besides waiting, voting itself may even take place outside to facilitate transparency (Willis et al. 2017). Participation is unavoidably public and provides a gathering where community members socialize.

The visibility of the process and open-air nature of waiting also allows actors beyond one's neighbors, like candidate agents, local authorities, and other brokers, to observe voting lines throughout the day in hopes that in areas of perceived support their presence encourages (and verifies) turnout. As Nichter (2008) describes in Argentina:

> Voting procedures ... make it far easier for the Peronists to monitor *whether* individuals vote. Party delegates are permitted within polling places (*mesas*) and are actually expected to supervise electoral officials as they record who shows up at their designated location. As Canton and Jorrat ... explain, "the mesa authorities, under supervision of the party delegates, write on the register list, beside the surname of the person who has just voted, in a special column, the word 'cast.'" Individuals' identity documents are signed and sealed to provide proof of voting, offering yet another way to monitor turnout. (21)

Verification is improved by the use of indelible ink applied to voters' fingers identifying them on election day – and days after – as having voted. Such inking is a usual and important innovation in many developing countries, because when lacking reliable electronic voter registration systems or electronic voting, ink prevents fraudulent double-voting. In some countries, citizens, candidates, and party agents can also directly observe polling station counts, like Ghana (Figure A.1.H) and Uganda (Figure C.3). Public posting of vote tallies by election officials after the count is often required by law (as in Afghanistan, Figure D.3), which allows community members to assess overall turnout and total vote shares. By seeing how many people voted from tallies, parties and agents can make plans about their distributive choices.

Because voting is visible on election day and after, communities can convey a reasonable expectation of monitoring over an extended window and pressure others to vote and identify defectors for possible sanctioning. Bus riders on election day in Egypt are often removed unless they show evidence of having voted with a marked index finger (Magdy 2019). In Zimbabwe, Robert Mugabe's supporters went door to door threatening "the most ferocious retribution" for voters without inked fingers (BBC 2008). For Indians, inability to display inking after election day can produce social scorn typically leveled at criminals, which explains "why on election day villagers discreetly checked out each other's fingers and made their surprise and disapproval known to those who as yet bore no mark" (Banerjee 2007: 1560). Beyond the fear of sanctioning driven by community expectations to vote, the visibility of the act motivates voters to turn out and enables them to show their community "I voted!" with a marked finger.[9]

2.3.3 Hypotheses

We now discuss the observable implications of our theory as derived from our ABM, including factors that are more likely to produce the puzzle of high turnout, where *both* V_1 and V_2 participate. Our framework predicts strong expectations and pressure to participate plus the monitoring capacity to verify turnout combines to generate perceptions of social sanctioning, a negative selective incentive and a critical contributor to mobilization. That is, the more likely someone believes the punishment for not doing an action will be applied, the more likely they are to perform the action; participation increases both as penalties for noncooperation and perceptions of monitoring capacity increase. While variation in perceptions of community expectations and monitoring capacity could independently affect turnout, their combined effect motivates participation further.

Social sanctioning therefore results in a negative payoff, which decreases the value (and net advantages) of staying home (Figure E.2). As penalties for staying home become bigger or more credible, the desire to avoid those penalties increases turnout likelihood. Our theory predicts that the magnitude of

---

[9] Visibility alone could inspire residents to participate not necessarily because they expect sanction, but because they want to signal their "type" (e.g., a contributor to community goods) to other community members. Neighbors signal this by voting, inducing a separating equilibrium that allows actions to distinguish contributing and noncontributing types. We do not discount this may explain some cooperative behavior, however we believe it is not contradictory to social sanctioning and may be subsumed by it. Revealing type through voting works if community members perceive the signal that way – only likely because the action is costly and widely considered to support the community's welfare. We also empirically observe the actual application of sanctioning. The expectation and perception of sanctioning matter even where actions alone could signal type.

social sanctions need not be particularly high to have a dramatic effect on participation; only a subset of the population needs to perceive sanctioning to increase turnout overall (Figure E.2). Because social sanctions must merely be perceived, even small changes in perception or application can create large changes in total turnout rates by tipping a few fence-sitters into voting that compounds the expectations for their neighbors. Our first hypothesis states:

H1: As an individual's perceptions of social sanctioning increases, so does their likelihood of electoral participation.

Our model also compares social sanctioning against alternative psychic and material motivations. Of course, these factors are not necessarily mutually exclusive from each other, or social sanctioning. Our approach allows it to be true that psychic and material incentives exist at baseline levels at the same time they are not overwhelmingly determinative of behavior – given that rates of ethnic voting and the scale and magnitude of incentives in the form of vote-buying would need to be significantly higher than what we have observed in emerging democracies to account fully for observed participation levels. This could partly explain the weak correlation between expressive and contingent motivations with turnout even in contexts with ethnic divisions and opportunities for patronage.

To explore why, as summarized from our model, voting to receive psychic benefits from expressing ethnic solidarity requires participation alongside co-ethnics with similar feelings. If voters place a high salience on expressing group affinity (independent of the source of salience), the benefits to turning out decrease as either affective ties or their salience decrease – equivalent to up-weighting, or providing a "bonus" for voting (or down-weighting staying home, Figure E.3). Strong ethnic affinity may change individuals' calculations from "stay home" to "participate" where the difference between the costs and benefits of participating is relatively small; however, such psychic incentives must be significantly large to overcome the direct and opportunity costs of not voting, and the weight of ethnic or other affective ties must be uniformly high across the population (and ethnic groups) to induce high observed turnout levels (Figure E.3).

Material considerations are also likely to be lower in magnitude. Vote-buying is provided by a party or candidate directly to an individual in exchange for turnout. Therefore, participation will be positively correlated with perceptions that voting is expected in exchange for a material benefit, equivalent to adding to the voter's expected payoff for participation. While vote-buying may change certain individuals' calculations from "stay home" to "participate" when the difference between the costs and benefits of voting is relatively small, private incentives must be large enough to overcome the direct and opportunity costs of not voting, and vote-buying must be distributed at very high rates across the population, to induce observed turnout levels (Figure E.4).

As a result, our second hypothesis contends that social sanctioning plays a significant role beyond ethnicity and vote-buying in making voting more likely:

H2: Relative to feelings of ethnic attachment or vote-buying, perceptions of social sanctioning are more likely to increase the likelihood of an individual's electoral participation.

Before extending our theory, we address some possible countervailing dynamics that could reasonably lessen the degree to which social sanctioning increases participation. While we observe some of these dynamics anecdotally in our cases and others, and they likely contribute at least somewhat to variation in turnout across contexts, we briefly explain why we do not think that they consistently undercut our generalized approach.

Communities could exclude certain residents from local services, such as those within their area who do not share their interests or are perceived as outsiders (like ethnic minorities), and as a result these individuals would be unlikely to perceive strong expectations to participate (and therefore may abstain or participate for other reasons). Although members of a majority group could pressure minority members to stay home, we do not believe this forms an effective suppression strategy in emerging democracies, where hyper-local polling station–level social group homogeneity is still high, national or regional diversity is not as likely to be reflected locally, and communities of voters are often almost entirely composed of members of the same group. Our cases further show that even in locally mixed areas or those with minority group members, ethnic demography does not consistently counteract the effects of social sanctioning. While we lack definitive evidence, we posit that people with shared interests in local areas, even if they include minorities, still have incentives and lend resources to pressure members of the community to vote to advance collective interests (in line with Ichino and Nathan's 2013 research from Ghana).[10]

Turnout may also stall when a political actor explicitly intimidates others, modeled as a "violence" cost in Table 1. While this could include an actual attack, such a deterrent can be generalized as a disincentive arising from the trauma of past violence or threat of future violence. At an individual level, the "violence" cost would intuitively decrease the likelihood of participation, but at

---

[10] Relatedly, Long and Gibson (2015) find local ethnic diversity in Kenya does not result in voters' attempts to exclude area minorities from receiving services, but rather they provide evidence that concentrated support among local (even diverse) communities helps elect politicians that deliver, results that echo Barkan (1997; see Section 3.3.3) and Barfield (2010; see Section 4.3).

the population level the existence of such a penalty does not consistently undermine the generally positive effects of social sanctioning, even as it declines for some individuals. Indeed, the literature offers mixed results of violence's effects on political behavior (echoed in our cases), suggesting context matters a great deal in how it shapes participatory behavior. But even if exposed to violence previously or threatened with intimidation, the pressure that community members place on "fence-sitters" could result in them conforming to socially desirable behavior.

Similarly, people might stay home because of an election boycott. Boycotts occur because (typically opposition) parties do not believe they can compete on an equal playing field (Beaulieu 2014), and then explicitly coordinate on preventing turnout. Although boycotts reduce participation levels, as we observe in Kenya (2017) and Afghanistan (2009), they still require successful collective action of the type our theory implies.

Finally, while monitoring helps enforce voting standards, capacity to monitor varies by context. As it becomes more difficult or citizens perceive it less, participation may not increase at the same rate. For example, election laws in Uganda require all voting and ballot counts to take place outside – facilitating easy monitoring (Figure C.3) – similar to Ghana, where most voting and counts are outdoors in areas easily accessed by community members (Figures A.1–2). But in Afghanistan, security protections to enter polling centers partially reduced visibility for nonvoters wishing to access them. We still document monitoring capacity in Section 4, but generally if factors like security protocols hinder observation, it is more difficult to verify specific individuals' turnout.

2.4 Extending the Theory: Social Capital and Trust

By focusing on the social origins shaping individual behavior, we explore an extension of our theory applied to conflict-prone, fragile democracies: whether variation in social capital influences the degree of social sanctioning necessary to induce cooperation. Studies document a robust relationship between social capital and trust (Fafchamps 2003). Trust has implications for political behavior and market exchanges: as social capital rises, groups coordinate better, for example to vote (Atkinson and Fowler 2014), because increased trust and communication help to compel shared practices and lower costs of in-group sanctioning. We relate this perspective to an active conflict setting, comprising the most vulnerable of contemporary developing democracies, because although trust shapes how well communities cooperate to enforce norms, variation from local dynamics – especially from persistent violence – could strengthen or attenuate social bonds. Divisions caused by prior or ongoing sectarian violence could erode trust and community cooperation in some locales. Alternatively, social capital and trust could strengthen due to shared traumatic events and encourage prosocial behavior.

We posit that the ease of turnout enforcement depends on extant social capital such that the strength of social sanctioning varies inversely with trust. This is because high trust communities have greater Olsonian endowments, or "reserves," to solve collective action problems. As trust increases, individuals are more cooperative and uphold norms independently – they require fewer sticks (sanctioning) since communities with higher levels of trust need fewer inducements to punish defectors, either because communities already exert so much perceived pressure to achieve cooperation or because the norms are so internalized that people do not require external pressure or monitoring. In contrast, communities with decreasing social capital have more difficulty coordinating and therefore require *more* pressure to enforce norms. Therefore, trust and social sanctioning are not substitutes; rather, as trust increases the need to impose sanctions decreases because baseline cooperation levels are already higher. While communities no doubt generate perceptions of sanctioning, perceptions matter most to those whose feelings of trust and social capital are lowest (e.g., those who might stay home).

Leveraging data collection from Afghanistan in Section 4, we explore the heterogeneous effects of individuals' trust of their neighbors on the likelihood they vote and hypothesize that:

H3: Higher levels of trust in one's neighbors decreases the magnitude of social sanctioning on an individual's likelihood of electoral participation.

2.5 Conclusion

Electoral mobilization creates a collective action problem that communities must overcome to support their interests. They do so by exerting strong social expectations to participate and rely on the visibility of voting to credibly monitor turnout. In countries with persistent instability and violence, individuals in communities with higher levels of baseline trust likely require less enforcement of norms to vote. In Sections 3 and 4, we investigate these implications empirically.

3 Testing the Theory in Africa's Third-Wave Democracies: Ghana, Kenya, and Uganda

Our first empirical exploration focuses on three recent African democratizers that provide good comparisons: Ghana, Kenya, and Uganda. All are former British colonies, achieved sovereignty in the same period, and share electoral systems, similar levels of ethnic diversity, and average income. Early democratic experiments after independence collapsed under their leaders' growing authoritarianism, but each transitioned during the third wave and has held elections since. Their citizens routinely express support for democracy, and psychic and material incentives – including the salience of ethnic identity, vote-buying, and electoral violence – have the potential to shape participation. So does social sanctioning, due to a variety of mechanisms that communities leverage to pressure members and monitor turnout.

These cases also have important differences that underscore the diversity of third-wave democracies, in particular their party systems. Because formal actors – like the government, candidates, and party agents – will matter for electoral mobilization, we aim to show how social sanctioning operates across party settings. Ghana, considered one of Africa's most successful democracies, has a two-party system, and both parties have alternated power. While Ghanaian elections are often close and swing voters decisive, the options are consistent. Ghana provides a starting point to explore turnout motivations in a stable, yet still competitive, environment. Kenya's party system is more volatile, with a plethora of small, localized, parties – many of which exist as electoral vehicles for local bosses in ethno-regional strongholds – that coordinate to support broad and ever-shifting national coalitions. Election outcomes are contentious and unpredictable. Uganda's dominant party system has a single machine that has always won the presidency and a majority of parliamentary seats. Elections are by-and-large foregone conclusions, but the opposition nonetheless manages vigorous campaigning.

Taken together, our cases sharpen the puzzle of turnout and individuals' motivations. While turnout varies, it has not consistently declined. Participation in Ghana's 1992 democratic transition was a modest 50 percent, shooting to 78 percent in 1996 and holding at 78 percent in 2020 during the pandemic. Campaign violence, human rights abuses, and protests have been routine in Kenyan elections. In 2007, when turnout was 69 percent, allegations of rigging culminated in six weeks of violence, leading to more than 1,000 civilians dead and nearly 700,000 displaced. But turnout reached 86 percent in 2013 and 80 percent in 2017. Ugandan rebel leader Yoweri Museveni took office in 1986 and, starting in 1996, allowed so-called "no-party" elections before legalizing multipartyism in 2006, when turnout hit 70 percent. Despite Museveni's National Resistance Movement always winning by healthy margins, turnout hovers above 60 percent, including in 2021, which saw violent opposition targeting and pandemic protocols at polling stations. These countries represent Africa well, but our aim is not to leverage institutional similarities and differences to test contrasting theoretical predictions in a manner relying on case variation. Rather, we hope to demonstrate that our hypotheses operate across cases considering these similarities and differences.

For Ghana (Section 3.1), Kenya (Section 3.2), and Uganda (Section 3.3), we first briefly review electoral background and provide descriptive evidence from ethnographic, administrative, and survey data sources to demonstrate how psychic and material incentives plausibly operate. Then we discuss presence and capacity for social sanctioning – community pressure and monitoring capabilities for turnout verification. A uniform structure highlights the contrasting evidence for general theoretical predictions, drawing on context-specific data and informed by our experience observing elections. Each case concludes with summaries of more systematic quantitative tests of our first two hypotheses using original survey data from recent elections (Appendix I, Sections A–C describe measures and present full results and robustness checks).

3.1 Ghana

3.1.1 Setting

Ghana (formerly Gold Coast) achieved independence from Great Britain in 1957. Kwame Nkrumah of the Convention People's Party served as prime minister (1957–1960) and then president (1960–1966). While initially popular, Nkrumah's government increasingly curtailed political opposition; following economic mismanagement and alleged corruption, the military overthrew him in 1966, initiating a succession of coups and unstable civilian governments. In 1979's "June 4th Revolution," Jerry Rawlings and other military officers seized control, their ruling council targeting many from the former political class while promising reform. Reflecting third-wave democratization across Africa, Rawlings acceded to multiparty elections in 1992.

Party systems in emerging democracies tend either toward fractionalization (like Kenya) or single-party dominance (like Uganda). Contrastingly, Ghana has two institutionalized parties, the National Democratic Congress (NDC) and New Patriotic Party (NPP). Both have won the presidency and a majority of parliamentary seats since 1992 through peaceful transfers of power. After serving as military dictator, Rawlings founded the NDC, winning the presidency in 1992 and 1996. John Kufuor's NPP defeated the NDC in 2000 and again in 2004. We observed elections in 2008, the first round (December 7) featuring the NPP's Nana Akufo-Addo against the NDC's John Atta Mills, who had served as Rawlings's vice president and run against Kufuor in 2000 and 2004.

The electoral rules dictate a runoff if no presidential aspirant garners at least 50 percent + 1 of votes, and legislators are elected from single-member simple-plurality constituencies, with the NDC and NPP garnering more than 90 percent of parliamentary seats. Recent presidential races have been exceptionally close. In 2008, Akufo-Addo was barely below the threshold (49.13% to Atta Mills's 47.92%), forcing a second round that Atta Mills won. Atta Mills died in office in 2012; his vice president John Mahama led the NDC to a 50.7/47.7 percent victory over Akufo-Addo in 2012. Akufo-Addo then won in 2016, with 54 percent, and again in 2020, with 51 percent.

Largely due to stable party dynamics and peaceful alternation, observers characterize Ghana as one of Africa's most successful democratizers – the only West African country the Economist Intelligence Unit's (2021) Democracy Index codes as a full democracy. Freedom House ranks it "free" (Repucci and Slipowitz 2021). Ghanaians overwhelmingly support democracy – in the first Afrobarometer (1999), 76 percent favored democracy compared to 9 percent favoring an alternative; in 2017, 81 percent of respondents preferred democracy.

Ghanaians' opinions about democracy do not easily translate into predictions about electoral behavior, however. In countries with consolidated party systems and alternation, turnout allegedly swells in transitional elections to then decline and level-off as they become routine. This pattern has not held in Ghana: 1992's participation was 50 percent, a low benchmark that has since varied but remained high: 70 percent in 2008 (and 73% in the second round) and 79 percent in 2020. As a consolidating African democracy with a stable party system, such strong turnout is surprising.

3.1.2 Psychic and Material Incentives

Why are Ghanaians such reliable voters? We apply psychic and material considerations to Ghana's electoral context to assess first the plausibility of intrinsic and extrinsic motivations.

A first perspective relates to mobilization tied to ethnicity. Ghana has avoided sustained ethnic conflict, but ethnicity is a tool for political organizing. To see why ethnic allegiance may inspire turnout, first consider Ghana's exceptional diversity (Table A.1). No ethnic group constitutes a majority. The broad Akan ethno-linguistic family accounts for 49 percent of the population, but within the Akan are several distinct groups like the Ashanti (or Asante) (15%), Akim (6%), and Fante (10%). Other larger groups are the Ewe (13%), Mole-Dagbani (15%), and Ga (8%); smaller ones comprise the remaining 15 percent.

Although not strictly ethnic parties since they draw membership from multiple groups, the NPP and NDC nonetheless have ethnic reputations. The NPP is perceived as having an Ashanti base because it receives backing from business interests in the central Ashanti region (surrounding the city of Kumasi) and southern Ghana, where many closely related Akan reside and were historically more integrated into the Gold Coast colonial economy. The NPP also recruits Ashanti and other Akan chiefs into party leadership. John Kufuor, the NPP standard-bearer in 2000 and 2004, is Ashanti; Nana Akufo-Addo, the NPP's erstwhile aspirant turned president since 2016, is Akim (close relatives of the Ashanti). Our 2008 exit poll (Table A.2) confirms strong NPP support from these groups: 83 percent of Ashanti voted for Akufo-Addo and 75 percent for the NPP parliamentary candidate; 75 percent of Akim chose Akufo-Addo and 72 percent voted NPP in parliament.

The NDC's ethnic orientation relates to Rawlings, an Ewe, a group that resides in eastern Volta. Rawlings founded the NDC, made it victorious through two elections, and continued to exert influence over party operations until his death in 2020. The Ewe have voted NDC in presidential and parliamentary races (72% and 70%, respectively, in 2008, Table A.2). Such support is not universal, but on par with associated groups' NPP alignment.

The mobilizing power of ethnicity for the NPP and NDC may not extend to other groups, at least not consistently. Given the electoral system, parties must garner votes beyond their ethnic enclaves. Groups often swing support across elections or divide their vote, including the north's Mole-Dagbani and the south's Ga. And despite the NDC's Ewe reputation, it has not nominated an Ewe for president recently. From 2000 to 2008, they ran Atta Mills, a Fante; in 2008, Ewe support for the NDC still held strong, although the Fante vote split (Table A.2). From 2012 to 2020, the NDC's standard-bearer was northerner John Mahama, from the small Gonja ethnicity group, who hold cultural ties to and residence near the Akan (and distant from the Ewe).

Given, and perhaps due to, these nuanced ethnic dynamics, Ghanaians do not express strong affective ties to their ethnic groups, and such sentiments do not consistently predict participation. To measure the degree of ethnic affinity, our 2008 pre-election survey asked respondents their language/ethnic group followed by: "Let us suppose you had to choose between being a Ghanaian and being a [insert name of language/ethnic group]. Which of these groups do you feel most strongly attached to?"[11] Six percent identified more with their ethnic rather than national identity (40% equally), but strong ethnic identifiers were no more or less likely to report intending to vote.[12] Further, in examining

---

[11] This question reflects Afrobarometer wording and how other scholars measure ethnic affinity (Robinson 2014).

[12] Given the partial intersection between ethnicity and partisanship, expressive voting could also be mediated through attachments to the NPP or NDC. But in our exit poll, only 46 percent felt "very" or "somewhat close" to a political party, and we find no statistical correlation between ethnic identifiers and feeling close to a political party in our pre-election survey.

2008 turnout by region (Table A.3), while Ashanti and Volta were the strongest ethnic vote-bank enclaves for the NPP and NDC with turnout of 74 percent and 67 percent, such levels did not differ significantly from northern swing areas (Northern (75%), Upper East (71%), and Upper West (69%)); or Accra (67%).

Perhaps, then, material incentives offered through vote-buying inspires Ghanaians? Our framework conceptualizes vote-buying as providing a net positive payoff, offsetting some (or all) costs of participation. Even though vote-buying is illegal and punishable by law, the susceptibility of Ghanaians to pecuniary rewards could be due to many voters' income status and the view, as elsewhere in Africa, that they expect handouts from politicians.[13] Vote-buying is allegedly so rampant that businesses complain that because elections are held in December, political gift-giving leaves citizens unable or unwilling to complete their Christmas shopping (VOA News 2009). Evidence suggests that recent increased urbanization and economic growth have not necessarily diminished the influence of patronage (Nathan 2019b). Although vote choice is private, contingent exchanges may prove self-enforcing in Ghana, where reciprocal norms are alleged to cause voters to uphold their end of the bargain (Lynge-Mangueira 2013).

There are also reasons to doubt that vote-buying, such as it exists, explains mass behavior. Only 7 percent of Round 5 Afrobarometer respondents reported having been offered a gift (food or money) in exchange for a vote. Our 2008 pre-election survey found that only 30 percent of respondents thought it was "very or somewhat important" for "political parties [to] reward their supporters with gifts and money in exchange for support" (Table A.4).[14] Vote-buying may not constitute an effective approach for swaying opinions as surveys suggest that voters' considerations of performance on the economy and public services helps candidates win (Hoffman and Long 2013). Since Rawlings' liberal reforms, the use of government employment for patronage has declined; the NDC overhauled its primary election procedures to minimize vote-buying (Ichino and Nathan 2022); and Akufo-Addo has gained NPP popularity in recent elections by running on an anti-corruption platform. Contingent exchanges may also not prove self-enforcing: "In Ghana, villagers have made a habit of accumulating tee-shirts from all the parties which happen to pass through . . .. [Voters] turn the tables on gullible politicians who imagine that expressions of interest signal a genuine intention to vote for them" (Nugent 2006: 257).

---

[13] 2008 GDP per capita was USD 1,217.

[14] This captures attitudes and expectations regarding vote-buying, not its actual level, reflecting our theory since contingent strategies only work if voters express a desire for or expectation of gifts in exchange for voting.

What about the potential for psychic or material costs related to violence? Electoral violence in Ghana is less of a threat compared to our other cases, and incidents are mostly isolated. During election years the average recorded events rose only marginally, from 14.3 to 19 (Bekoe and Burchard 2017). On our pre-election survey, 14 percent replied that they thought violence was very or somewhat likely in their communities on election day (Table A.4). Intimidation is more common, with 44 percent of Round 5 Afrobarometer respondents expressing fear of becoming a victim of political intimidation or violence during the campaign. Strong turnout nonetheless persists.

3.1.3 Social Sanctioning

We now review evidence to investigate aspects of social sanctioning, which includes perceiving both community pressure to vote and monitoring capacity based on its visibility.

We first look to Ghanaians' views of the government's responsibility to provide services to assess the potential for pressure. Overwhelmingly, the government is seen as an important source of public goods. To our pre-election survey question, "Who is mainly responsible for delivering services *in your community*?" 32 percent of respondents replied the central government, 35 percent responded MPs, and 28 percent responded assemblyperson – all elected officials. This is not surprising; historically, Ghanaians regard the government as needing to take actions to address problems of welfare and the economy. Nkrumah adopted "developmental" planning, and Rawlings maintained approval by making populist economic appeals at the same time as effectuating free-market policies that helped economic growth. Today, while the NDC portrays itself as somewhat left of center and the NPP burnishes its business-friendly reputation, both legislate and campaign on promises of economic management and improving services (Harding 2015). Because voting has important implications for policy and service delivery, voters are sensitive to government actions affecting their communities.

Accordingly, Ghanaians express strong beliefs that fellow citizens should vote. In the Round 6 Afrobarometer, asked how often a "good citizen" in a democracy votes, 85 percent said "always" and 13 percent "only if they so choose." Elections are celebrations and community affairs, drawing in neighbors and area residents. As a sign of the potential for perceptions of social sanctioning, our pre-election poll asked a question probing community expectations to vote: "Thinking about elections in Ghana, how important is it for everyone in your community to vote, even if they do not like the candidates?" 66 percent replied "very important" (Table A.4).[15]

---

[15] We specified undesirable candidates to minimize the utility gained from differences of policy/ ideological positions, *B* in Riker and Ordeshook. When voters gain utility from their ideological

Beyond their NDC and NPP affiliations, local MPs are personally identifiable, another indication that grassroots collective action could work to drive locals the polls. According to a survey by Cheeseman, Lynch, and Willis (2021), 67 percent of Ghanaians could correctly name their MP, and linkages between politicians and communities "animates the relationship between candidates and voters" (73). In interviews with MPs, the authors report that politicians and party leaders understand the importance of attending to constituency services:

> As one politician told us, to campaign is to invite demands for assistance . . . .
> These demands may be individual – *but they are often collective, cast in the language of community and development:* ' . . . they want electricity, they want hospitals and clinics and their roads [quoting a politician in Volta]' (ibid., emphasis added).

MPs are often responsive to voter demands as measured through the former's spending on constituency development funds. Given the expectation of either NPP or NDC victories and because of close ties with local politicians, many voters reasonably want to support the winning coalition and believe it matters for the services their communities receive. Just as local leaders are "shamed into action" when they do not act in the community's best interests (Paller 2019:139), so too communities use expectations of reciprocity to drive participation.

To enforce community turnout further, numerous other actors promote and facilitate collective action and legitimize participation in formal institutions. Civil society, parties, and community organizations have long targeted women and youths to galvanize their electoral participation and that of their households.

The two national parties play an important role organizing and mobilizing a diverse set of voters. National competitiveness has raised the stakes of electoral strategies, aiding in parties' professionalization, although neither the NPP nor NDC is equally strong everywhere. They exert the most capacity driving turnout in their vote-banks while attempting to capture swing constituencies through ties to local authorities, such as traditional chiefs, who promise votes in exchange for personal connections to power. Both Ashanti chiefs and those from the north have flexed influence in national politics, often linking key constituencies to local and national political centers (Nathan 2019a). Even as the state provides many area services, chiefs are important in delivering local

---

closeness to a candidate's position, B increases and potentially offsets D – however this remains conditional on p, the probability that the person's vote proves decisive, which is still effectively zero. Phrasing the question with respect to "candidates you do not like" gives us empirical leverage on a condition that forces a minimum of utility gained from B. With $pB+D>C$, this mechanically reduces B to zero if, for whatever reason, voters actually misperceive p. Then focusing on $D>C$, we impute intrinsic and extrinsic motivations in D through $D=U(DI, DE)$ following Gerber, Green, and Larimer (2008); another way to view this is by reducing the net value of C.

order and mediating disputes between residents. Another avenue of pressure occurs through religious leaders. Ghanaians are deeply religious; most are either Christian (71%) or Muslim (20%). Due to the centrality of religion in everyday life, preachers and imams oversee collective action, uphold community standards, and admonish nonbelievers or those who violate customs. Religious leaders routinely summon residents to vote to support democracy, abjure violence, and to "pray for a peaceful outcome" to elections; churches arrange for their members to observe the vote and count.

In urban areas, additional brokers, or "opinion leaders," forge connections between communities and government institutions (Klaus and Paller 2017). They aid in voter mobilization by serving as "political muscle" for candidates and parties – often a steppingstone to running for office themselves (Paller 2019). Reliant on support in exchange for networking disconnected communities to public goods, an Accra resident acknowledged they were well aware that their local broker "would be causing lots of problems" if the community did not mobilize to support his efforts during elections (ibid.:154).

Vote choice is private but voting itself is rather public, as we witnessed, enabling community monitoring of turnout. Polling centers host a few hundred to a few thousand voters, who reside in the surrounding community. Figure A.1 shows an Accra polling station we visited, outside in a yard next to a school. In Panel A, voters have allowed those who with disabilities to sit at the front of the line, and in Panel B, they are waiting patiently for the polling center to open. One should assume visible queuing. Panels C-E demonstrate the actual voting process, observable to anyone present. Outside of the school compound, Panel F shows a lengthy formation gathered along the street. Anybody who drives or walks by can easily see who is in line (Panel G). Figure A.2 represents similar dynamics in a rural polling station in Cape Coast, a communal yard outside a school, with Panels A–C indicating a long line in early afternoon.

Security personnel and party representatives are present during balloting; over 62,000 officers and 4,000 agents were deployed to polling stations in 2020 (Kokutse 2020). Parties and civil society organizations also routinely oversee voting and the count to report irregularities.[16] Indeed, the allowances for poll watchers directly support turnout monitoring by placing NDC and NPP agents, and their affiliated personnel, at most centers. While 81 percent in our exit poll sample perceived their ballot to be secret (which should be true by law), those who perceived a violation were in areas where parties demonstrated stronger organization (Ferree and Long 2016). In Figure A.1 Panel H, we witnessed

---

[16] While extensive fraud is uncommon, elections remain contentious and closely fought in many areas.

residents of the Labone neighborhood in Accra gathering to watch count proceedings during the evening. Monitoring how local areas voted is additionally visible via public tally posting after the count.

Finger marking also allows verification. The pride associated with the visual display of electoral participation has come to be known as exercising the "power of the thumb" (Figure A.3), with images of inked fingers shared widely online. Ghanaians without marking are perceived to have abstained. In 2008, the domestic monitoring consortium reported ink used at 93 percent of stations. Party representatives and community members often "help out" with the voting process and inking: an official from the Center for Democratic Development noted, "[Sometimes] election workers and registration officials are so overwhelmed with work that they allow party people to ... help them out, such as inking the finger for registrants who have been processed, or even allowing the registrants and observers to be so close to them as to access all the information on the voters" (Larvie 2008). In 2020, a rumored lack of ink in Ayawaso West Wuogon constituency caused brief panic; a local candidate and local residents pleaded to pause voting until ink could arrive (Graphic Online 2020), prompting a formal response from the election commission.

3.1.4 Quantitative Analysis

We briefly summarize statistical exercises that more formally test our hypotheses with nationally representative household survey data of registered Ghanaian voters a few weeks before the December 2008 election.[17] Simple differences-of-means (Table A.5) show that a respondent who did not perceive pressure to vote by community members, a proxy for social sanctioning, had a 71 percent likelihood of voting, which increases to 79 percent when they do perceive pressure ($p<0.01$). We find no statistically significant difference in ethnic identifiers reporting intent to vote. Those who report expectations of vote-buying are slightly less likely to vote, and those who predict violence are thirteen points less likely to vote ($p<0.01$). In multivariate tests controlling for relevant sociodemographic and political variables (Table A.6), social sanctioning is significant and positive across different model specifications: as voters' beliefs about the importance of their community members voting increases, so does their own likelihood of voting, by four to five percentage points. Coefficients for ethnic identifiers and those who believe supporters should be rewarded with material goods are not well estimated; neither is expecting violence.

---

[17] 2,033 respondents; Appendix A provides the survey methodology for quantitative tests, codings, descriptive statistics, and robustness checks.

Bolstered by other accounts from Ghana, these statistical tests are positive, if still suggestive, evidence in support of our first two hypotheses. Diverse factors no doubt enter the calculation of Ghanaians' decision to vote, including communities' desire to turn out members and monitor who participates. Relative to feelings of ethnic attachment or vote-buying, perceptions of social sanctioning may increase individuals' participation and overall turnout across the population. Does evidence from Kenya corroborate these findings?

3.2 Kenya

3.2.1 Setting

Kenya became independent from Britain in 1963. The Kenya African National Union (KANU), led by Jomo Kenyatta, was the dominant political force and won elections in the 1960s. Kenyatta's leadership became increasingly autocratic, establishing a de facto one-party state. Unlike Ghana, Kenya never experienced a successful military coup, and unlike Uganda, it never experienced widespread civil conflict. Upon Kenyatta's death (1978), vice president Daniel arap Moi assumed office, revised the constitution in 1982 to inscribe a de jure one-party state under KANU, and cracked down on opposition leaders. After a wave of civil society activism and international pressure, Moi removed legal restrictions against multipartyism in 1991. Like Rawlings and the NDC, Moi and KANU won transitional elections in 1992 and again in 1997 – but with only pluralities against divided oppositional factions. Allegations of rigging for KANU in some parliamentary races and campaign violence cast these elections as contentious and destabilizing.

Kenya's party system is unconsolidated and fractionalized. Parties typically arise initially from prominent leaders in ethno-regional strongholds, particularly around nominations for primaries and local seats, which then coalesce to endorse and mobilize voters in support of national tickets for presidential aspirants. While KANU had been dominant with Kenyatta and Moi, it is now mostly defunct. Due to term limits, Moi did not run in 2002, when a unified opposition National Rainbow Coalition (NARC) under Mwai Kibaki received 62 percent of the vote against Moi's anointed KANU successor, Uhuru Kenyatta (Jomo's son). Since 2002, viable presidential tickets have featured two broad nationwide, but ever evolving, coalitions sharing more than 90 percent of the presidential vote (Long 2020). An array of smaller, more local affiliated parties have won nearly all parliamentary seats.

In 2005, Kibaki's NARC government split following disagreement over a failed constitutional referendum and coalition defections, including by Raila Odinga, who formed the Orange Democratic Movement (ODM) and ran against

Kibaki's newly formed Party of National Unity in the December 2007 race. A third candidate, Kalonzo Musyoka of a splinter ODM-Kenya, contested as well but only received 10 percent of the vote to Kibaki's 46 percent and Odinga's 44 percent. Evidence of vote rigging sparked significant postelection violence between Odinga and Kibaki's supporters into early 2008 (Kanyinga et al. 2010). The dispute ended after international mediation led by Kofi Annan created a power-sharing Government of National Unity with Kibaki as president, Odinga prime minister, and Musyoka vice president.

Kenya is a presidential system; since the 2013 election (under a new constitution promulgated in 2010), presidential candidates must win 50 percent +1 (with the possibility of a runoff) and at least 25 percent of the vote in 24 of 47 counties. Presidential and parliamentary elections (with single-member simple-plurality rules) are held concurrently. Odinga's ODM has remained a strong machine in his regional enclave and placed him on a presidential ticket since 2007. Odinga has been allied with Musyoka and his rebranded "Wiper" Democratic Movement. Musyoka joined Odinga as deputy presidential candidate under a Coalition for Reforms and Democracy (CORD) alliance in 2013 and National Super Alliance (NASA) in 2017. In 2013, Uhuru Kenyatta's recently fashioned The National Alliance (TNA) and William Ruto's United Republican Party (URP) ran on a Jubilee Alliance ticket. Kenyatta had run against Kibaki in 2002, endorsed him in 2007, and held powerful ministerial positions under Kibaki's power-sharing regime. Ruto had been a strong ODM ally in 2007 but then fell out with Odinga as both worked in the unity government. Kenyatta's TNA and Ruto's URP officially merged into the Jubilee Party in advance of the 2017 race.

With a carousel of party and coalition alignments and names, election outcomes are hard to predict ex ante. In 2013 (the election we observed), Kenyatta/Ruto as Jubilee beat Odinga/Musyoka as CORD with 50.51 percent, narrowly avoiding a runoff despite Odinga's claims of rigging. In 2017, although the incumbents Kenyatta and Ruto were the certified first-round winners against Odinga/Musyoka's NASA, Odinga petitioned the result to the Supreme Court, which nullified the election based on technical deficiencies and called for a revote. Claiming a fair race was impossible, NASA boycotted the redo and established a "shadow" administration that refused to recognize Kenyatta/Ruto's re-election. With echoes of 2007–8, this plunged the country into political uncertainty, but Odinga eventually backed down after a widely derided "handshake" with Kenyatta, presaging Kenyatta's endorsement of Odinga over his deputy president Ruto when Odinga and Ruto squared off against each other in 2022. With ODM and other associates, Odinga led the Azimio La Umoja coalition against Ruto's United Democratic Alliance (UDA), which by then had split from Jubilee and Kenyatta but had allied with other parties under a newly formed Kenya Kwanza coalition. Ruto defeated Odinga with just a hair over the 50 percent threshold. Odinga petitioned the results again, but the Supreme Court rejected his claims and Ruto was duly inaugurated in September 2022.

Given the polarizing, often corrupt, and sometimes violent nature of elections, many scholars label Kenya a "hybrid" (semi-democratic) regime (Levitsky and Way 2010). Freedom House codes it "partly free" (Repucci and Slipowitz 2021). Citizens by and large register significant support for democracy: in its first Afrobarometer (2003), 80 percent of respondents preferred democratic over nondemocratic regime alternatives; in 2016, this support fell to 67 percent – perhaps indicating dissatisfaction with the candidate/coalition options.

Turnout rates vary but are impressive: 1992's race had 67 percent participation and 1997's rose to 83 percent. Turnout declined to 57 percent in 2002, but increased to 69 percent in 2007 and 86 percent in 2013, despite the postelection violence from 2007 to 2008. Turnout was 80 percent in 2017's first round (dropping in the revote to 39% due to Odinga's successful boycott and turnout limited to Jubilee supporters) and dipped to 65 percent in 2022.

3.2.2 Psychic and Material Incentives

What explains Kenyans' rather robust electoral participation? The country boasts a high degree of ethnic diversity, and ethnicity has shaped the political development of the country before and after multiparty transition. The Kikuyu constitute a plurality with about 21 percent (alongside the closely related Meru and Embu, at 5% and 1%), and are seen as politically dominant.[18] Like Ghana's Ashanti, Kikuyus were closely integrated (and exploited) into patterns of British colonial settlement, around central Kenya. Jomo and Uhuru Kenyatta and Mwai Kibaki are all Kikuyus, meaning the group has held the presidency every year since 1963, except for Daniel arap Moi's tenure (1978–2002) and now Ruto's (starting 2022). Moi and Ruto's ethnic Kalenjin (9–11%) are also formidable, often either aligned with or in opposition to the Kikuyu. Moi used his presidency to reward Kalenjin areas in Rift Valley. Kalenjins voted against Kibaki in 2007 – when Ruto endorsed Odinga – but then voted with Kenyatta in 2013 and 2017, when Ruto was Kenyatta's running mate. Much of the electoral violence in the 1990s and 2007–8 occurred between Kikuyus and Kalenjins such that the Kenyatta–Ruto pact was in large part driven by self-preservation: both had allegations against them

---

[18] Kenya conducts censuses routinely, but the government has not released ethnic breakdowns since 1989. Estimates here reflect that census and likely changes in ethnic proportions revealed in recent nationally representative surveys (see also Horowitz and Long 2016).

(eventually dismissed) at the International Criminal Court for directing post-election violence. Their coalition brought large swaths of voters from their communities to support Jubilee in 2013 and 2017 (Wamai 2020). In 2022, Kenyatta endorsed Odinga over Ruto, but both Odinga and Ruto had Kikuyu running mates.

Odinga's Luo (11%) mostly reside in Nyanza region near Lake Victoria and are another politically influential group, either aligned with or opposed to both Kikuyus and Kalenjins in recent elections. Kenyatta's first vice president was Jaramogi Odinga (Raila's father), who was eventually expelled from KANU. Father and son were seen as anti-KANU reformers, and Raila campaigned heavily against KANU in favor of NARC in 2002, and he has been on national tickets since 2007 (though never victorious). Musyoka hails from the Kamba (10%), who live in the eastern region and have also shifted alliances across election rounds, but mostly settling with Odinga from 2013 to 2022.

The salience of these ethnic dynamics becomes apparent viewing Table B.1, which displays vote choice by ethnicity from our 2013 exit poll. Bold-faced groups had a candidate on a viable national slate. In total, 83 percent of Kikuyus (and 75% of Merus) voted for Kenyatta, as did 74 percent of Kalenjins; 94 percent of Luos aligned with Odinga, along with 63 percent of Kambas. While levels of support vary, they demonstrate mostly ethnic alignment for those with co-ethnics on presidential tickets.

While these ethnic groups play musical chairs in forming national alliances, others are seen as more up for grabs, including the Luhya (14%) from western Kenya, Mijikenda (6%) from the coast, Somalis (3–4%) in northeastern, Maasai (2%) from Rift Valley, and Kisii (6%) in Nyanza. Table B.1 shows that these groups were more likely to split support between tickets. This is not surprising due to the constitutional stipulation requiring winning presidential aspirants to meet a minimum threshold of a quarter of the vote in at least 24 of 47 counties, forcing candidates to make appeals across diverse regions. For example, while Somalis only make up 3–4 percent of the total population, they constitute more than 90 percent in the ten counties of the northeast, positioning them as an influential swing vote.

To the extent that voters participate to express pride in their ethnicity, or resentment toward others, we would expect expressed ethnic affinity. But only 3 percent of our survey respondents in 2013 reported they felt closer to their ethnic group than to being Kenyan (Table B.2; 19% felt equally). Turnout in 2013 was significant nationwide, and some swing areas were as high as the ethnic vote banks for Jubilee and CORD (Long et al. 2013)

Even though vote-buying is illegal, Kenyans are potentially susceptible to material incentives to vote for specific candidates.[19] Increased urbanization, economic growth, and educational attainment since Moi left office have not necessarily minimized the perception that many votes in Kenya are bought. John Githongo, Kibaki's own former anti-corruption czar, lamented seeing "cash, T-shirts, and food" exchanged during 2002's election (Githongo 2007). Pecuniary giveaways are often the largest budget items for political candidates, and contingent exchanges may be self-enforcing if reciprocity norms inspire voters to uphold promises to politicians (Erlich 2020).

Nonetheless, civil society activists have attempted to crack down on election bribes, and direct reports of vote-buying are not too common. 66 percent of Afrobarometer (Round 5) respondents report "never" having been offered money or a gift in exchange for their vote; in our 2013 pre-election survey, only 8 percent report they had already been offered (one month before the election) money or gifts to vote for a particular candidate (Table B.2). Vote-buying is not always an effective strategy to sway voters: Kramon (2016) finds such practices influence the behavior of only around 23 percent of the elector-ate; surveys show that voters select candidates based on other considerations, such as providing public services – key to Kibaki's re-election in 2007 (Long and Gibson 2015) – and promising policy reforms – key to both Kenyatta and Odinga's popularity in 2013 (Ferree et al. 2014).[20]

Election violence periodically occurs in Kenya, although it does not appear to keep many voters home. Incumbents and parties engaged in pre-and/or post-election violence during the KANU era and in some elections since. The geographic concentration of ethnic groups into regional enclaves has resulted in fighting against those perceived as outsiders and between political factions in mixed areas. Such violence has included intimidation, land evictions, targeted killings of candidates or party agents, and other human rights abuses (CIPEV 2008). Postelection violence was a problem after disputed results in 2007, leading to six weeks of fighting between Kibaki's and Odinga's followers, during which more than 1,200 were killed and 700,000 displaced – and again in 2017, when there were dozens of attacks before and after the Supreme Court nullification of the election. The election we observed in 2013 was compara-tively more peaceful, but two insurgent groups – the Mombasa Republican Council and Al-Shabaab – committed pre-election attacks, threatening (unsuc-cessfully) to shut down voting. In our pre-election survey that year, 40 percent reported that violence had occurred in their communities in the previous (2007)

---

[19] Annual GDP per capita in 2013 was USD 1,354.

[20] Evidence demonstrates that voters will even reject co-ethnic candidates who they perceive to have not performed well (Ferree et al. 2021).

election, and 23 percent said they had personally been targets; 21 percent predicted election violence was "very" or "somewhat" likely to occur in their community in 2013 (Table B.2), and 15 percent said it had already. Despite these grim statistics, 2013 saw an increase of turnout to 86 percent from 69 percent in 2007.

3.2.3 Social Sanctioning

We now consider whether Kenyans plausibly face pressure to vote and monitored turnout.

Despite its historically uneven success, Kenyans nonetheless view the government as a critical source for public goods that helps meet subsistence in their day-to-day lives and for their communities. As shown across Afrobarometers and other surveys during election periods, Kenyans understand that government action, from national to local levels, affects local service delivery, including security, education, clinics, roads, and clean water (Long 2012). Kibaki rode an anti-KANU wave in 2002 in part due to Moi's economic mismanagement and corruption. By 2007, Kibaki received plaudits for achieving a robust growth rate and improvements in public services, specifically primary education (Gibson and Long 2009). Even after the 2007–8 election debacle, Kibaki left office in 2013 with a technocrat's legacy. From 2013 to 2022, Kenyatta succeeded at further economic reforms, and much of Jubilee's appeal revolved around its (perhaps ironic) promise to deliver better security and a "peaceful election" in 2013 (Odote 2020). Odinga has campaigned since 2007 on tackling unemployment and helping the gains from economic growth redound to previously marginalized areas. Ruto tried to undercut this strategy in 2022 by running on a "bottom-up" economic platform geared to his so-called "hustler nation" of the poor and youths.

Perhaps for these reasons, Kenyans report a strong expectation that others should participate in elections. In Afrobarometer Round 6, when asked how often a good citizen in a democracy votes, 89 percent said "always." Voting takes place in an environment of both communal celebration and anxiety. Close elections and fraud allegations in 2007 and 2017 resulted in protests, and all races since 2007 have been decided by small margins and disputed by Odinga.

Even given multiple, shifting coalitions, the individual identities of local officials are well known. Long (2012) finds that more than 90 percent of voters could correctly name their MP. Politicians understand the need to attend to constituency services, such as development projects, in a robust manner to prove popular among constituents (Young 2009), which tracks with how MPs spend constituency development funds (Harris and Posner 2019).

Many local actors promote and aid collective action, endorsing community participation in formal politics. Gender and family dynamics influence electoral behavior. Although Kenya is in many ways a patriarchal society, women's participation has long been a hallmark of public life. Women assist campaigns by cooking food for meetings and mobilizing household members and neighbors on election day. Women-led community groups are also important conduits to express the community's needs to candidates and identify female aspirants to run in local races. After the Supreme Court's nullification of Jubilee's 2017 victory, women in Nyeri, a Kenyatta stronghold, reportedly organized to drive their husbands to turn out for the revote by threatening to withhold sex if they did not (Dupuy 2017).

While parties are not nationally strong, they are important vehicles for candidates at the local level (Oloo 2020) – especially true of what Odinga has built for ODM, Musyoka for ODM-Kenya/Wiper, Kenyatta for Jubilee, and Ruto for UDA. These parties are no doubt vital for accumulating energy for national tickets, but they also coordinate votes for parliamentary and county races by registering voters, managing primaries, and mobilizing members to the polls. Parties are often associated with and financed by powerful local bosses, their families, businesses, and communities, and rely on all manner of brokers to organize for elections.

Additional players serve important roles greasing connections between communities and candidates, and often serve as a barometer for politicians' support – such as chiefs, elders, and community notables. Unlike Ghana and Uganda, chiefs in Kenya are an administrative (not traditional) designation (held over from the colonial period), who "served as central figures in the formation and implementation of state bureaucracy. With key roles, such as the dissemination and interpretation of government policies, enforcement of law and order ... and mobilization of political support, chiefs are considered a central part of the Kenyan state at the grassroots level" (Osborn 2020: 297). Local ethnic leaders similarly contribute important sources of community mobilization, including messages to coordinate on certain candidates during primaries or the general election, galvanizing the community's turnout on election day and colluding with other leaders on who should contest specific elected positions. Mitullah (2015) relays elite-led harmonization among the Kuria and Luos in Migori County:

> [A] local leader, was of the opinion that the Kuria should be given the posts of Senator and Deputy Governor as a demonstration of desire of unity in the county. In response, [Raila] Odinga urged the local leaders to form a negotiation committee .... [and] suggested that the aspirants all vie on ODM tickets to make work easy. This was a strategy for reducing inter-party competition and threat from other parties (351).

Kenyans are also deeply religious; 86 percent are Christian and 11 percent Muslim. Religious leaders have retained authority as arbiters of social norms, having helped lead the pro-democracy push in the 1990s. Today, politicians seek religious leaders' endorsements via the latter's attendance at political rallies, or through the former's attendance at large revivals and "prayer meetings." Churches perform voter outreach and coordinate to observe balloting and counts.

Other structures have co-evolved and fused with state institutions to articulate local service demands, such as the tradition of holding *barazas* – open-air public meetings often hosted by local elites – and *harambees* ("all pull together"), referring to local collective action to raise funds for development projects, like building a new school, often organized by community leaders and candidates.

Given the free-wheeling, competitive nature of Kenyan elections and the reliance of candidates on a plethora of local community representatives to muster electoral support, we suspect the activities of these actors and brokers likely reflect dynamics contributing to possible perceptions of social sanctioning. In wave 1 of our 2013 pre-election survey, we asked respondents if they had been personally contacted by any political agents during the campaign: 20 percent replied yes (Table B.2), and a further 50 percent reported that specifically candidates or their agents had actively encouraged them to vote.

Turnout is easy to verify. Centers that serve important community gathering points – schools, religious institutions, and fairgrounds – also function as polling centers. Much actual ballot filling occurs inside (typically an individual classroom), but it can also occur outside in tents erected in green spaces (Figure B.3). Even when voting inside a classroom, people line up outside for a long time in schoolyards under alphabetical listings of their designated "stream" (Figure B.4). To manage overcrowding, officials limit queue length within polling center compounds, often resulting in lines along roads outside the center. Kenyans routinely report having to wait hours to vote, first outside the compound and then in their streams (France 24 2017). The first polling center we visited in 2013 was Westlands Primary School, in a relatively wealthy area of Nairobi. The center hosted about 9,800 registered voters (unusually large) across 14 streams. We arrived 30 minutes before voting commenced, and the queue outside the school compound was already about two kilometers long (Figure B.1). Inside, voters waited adjacent to their stream (Figure B.2). At 1:30 p.m., we visited a center (located outside a mosque) in the (poorer) neighborhood of Eastleigh. Voters who had made it to their streams reported that they had lined up before 6 a.m. and still had not voted. Before 5 p.m., we observed a polling center at fairgrounds in Kibera, where voters were still waiting in long lines in front of tents (Figure B.3).

Beyond the ability of area residents to observe turnout, party agents and civil society organizations observe voting and the count at polling stations to report any irregularities. Though election manipulation is not uncommon, 92 percent of our exit poll respondents reported their ballot was secret, but in areas of strong ethnic support – particularly representing presidential tickets – local dynamics are such that those working to turn out the vote often put "intense pressure" on community members (Burbidge 2014). Because agents are allowed to observe balloting, they are frequently present on election day and capable of viewing who turns out. In 2013, domestic monitors reported party representatives at 98 percent of stations. While counts are restricted to election officials, certified observers, and parties, local tallies are visible immediately after, allowing the community and other agents to see how a precinct voted (Figure B.6).

Fingers are inked with permanent marker, making turnout choices visible for days (Figure B.5). As social media becomes more accessible, it has enabled voters to display their inked fingers with hashtags like "#KenyaDecides" to encourage other voters and avoid opprobrium (Musambi 2017). Martha Karua, Odinga's deputy presidential candidate, tweeted a picture of her inked finger after voting in 2022 (Figure B.7). Among other businesses, bars often withhold alcohol and other services from patrons unable to present finger marking on election day (Gachuhi 2017, cited in Harris 2021). In areas where agents rally support for specific candidates, voting becomes a matter of personal safety, with one resident recalling "if they don't see you voted by the ink on your finger, they beat you up" (Mari 2019). Public transportation vehicles will often not allow people to board unless they show a voter's card or inked finger. Inking is so common that polling officials have marked infants' fingers due to the proliferation of "babies-for-rent" scams, which enables voters to exploit a rule allowing mothers to cut lines if they are holding babies (Ndiso 2017).

3.2.4 Quantitative Analysis

Similar to Ghana, we conclude our discussion of Kenya by summarizing quantitative tests with survey data, specifically a third-wave panel from the 2013 election.[21] Looking at differences in means (Table B.3), average turnout for those who were contacted by political agents during the campaign, a proxy for social sanctioning, is two points higher than those who were not contacted

---

[21] The survey had about 4,500 respondents, with two pre-and one postelection waves, and roughly a 97 percent panel recontact rate. Our analysis pulls from wave 1, about one month before the election. Data, methodology, descriptive statistics, tests, and robustness checks are detailed in Appendix B.

(p<0.01), likely only a slight increase in magnitude since reported levels of intention to vote at 95 percent were already high, albeit not far off the certified level of 86 percent. We see no statistical difference in turnout among strong ethnic identifiers. Turnout among those who reported vote-buying is 1.5 percentage points less (p<0.1), and three percentage points less (p<0.01) among those who expect violence. Confirmed in multivariate tests (Table B.4), our independent variable of social sanctioning is significant and positively predicts turnout across model specifications with and without sociodemographic and political controls. As voters' contact with local parties increases, so does their likelihood of turning out (by about two percentage points, p<0.01). Coefficients for ethnic identifiers and vote-buying are not well estimated, but violence is negative and significant (reducing turnout by approximately 2.5 percentage points, p<0.01).

Statistical tests from Kenya, alongside other primary and secondary data, provide further confirmation of our first two hypotheses. Despite different party settings, Ghanaian and Kenyan elections are always lively affairs with robust participation. What about Uganda, where the same party always dominates? Why do Ugandans bother to vote?

3.3 Uganda

3.3.1 Setting

Uganda attained independence from Britain in 1962. Milton Obote of the Uganda People's Congress took office, but like Nkrumah and Jomo Kenyatta, he quickly turned dictatorial. In 1971 army commander Idi Amin toppled Obote in a coup. Under Amin, extensive reports documented arbitrary arrests, torture, and repressive killings of between 80,000 and 500,000 civilians. The Uganda National Liberation Front, with the backing of Tanzania's army, overthrew Amin in 1979 and established a transitional government. Obote made a comeback by winning elections in 1980, but allegations of rigging and resistance to another Obote regime prompted various guerilla factions to take up arms, including Yoweri Museveni's National Resistance Army (NRA). Obote's second term (1980–85) proved destabilizing again by failing to balance sectarian alliances or defeat the NRA. A 1985 coup ousted Obote in advance of the government's loss to the NRA, after which Museveni assumed the presidency in 1986 under a National Resistance Movement (NRM) government. In the 1990s, he allowed "no-party," or "movement," elections in which candidates contested independently for NRM seats. Against domestic and international calls for lifting the ban on parties, Museveni held a constitutional referendum in 2005, approved by 92 percent of voters, paving the way for multiparty elections in 2006.

Unlike Ghana or Kenya, a single party (NRM) has dominated the Ugandan government at national and many local levels since 1986. Museveni claimed political parties were responsible for the ills of postindependence politics as a justification for allowing no-party elections at the same time as he consolidated NRM hegemony through the 1990s. This strategy also relied on the formalization of former Resistance Councils (from the civil war period) into Local Councils (LCs), which now serve as focal points for political participation from the village to district levels. Today, the NRM is neither regionally based nor ideological in orientation – rather, it operates as a powerful nationwide machine.

Uganda's electoral rules match Ghana and Kenya's: two-round majority vote runoff for president and single-member simple-plurality rules for concurrent legislative elections. Museveni has won all four multiparty presidential elections decisively (2006, 2011, 2016, 2021); since 2006, no other candidate has garnered more than about 38 percent of the presidential vote. In 2006, Museveni won just under 60 percent (67% going to NRM MPs), rising in 2011 to 68 percent. Museveni received 61 percent in 2016 and 58 percent in 2021 (Table C.1).

Views of presidential elections and many parliamentary seats as foregone conclusions nevertheless masks some ways the system provides the appearance of competitive dynamics – both as Museveni tries to neutralize threats to NRM and the strategies candidates employ in various races. Two candidates have mounted somewhat viable challenges in recent presidential contests. The Forum for Democratic Change (FDC), led by Kizza Besigye, a former NRA member who had served as Museveni's physician, regularly obtained about a fourth to a third of the presidential vote in elections from 2006 to 2016, but FDC members routinely faced intimidation and abuse at the hands of the government. In 2021, a new challenger emerged: the singer-turned-politician, Robert Kyagulanyi Ssentamu, stage name "Bobi Wine," thirty-eight years old at the time of the election (Museveni was seventy-six). Wine's National Unity Platform won about 35 percent by running on a populist "throw the dinosaurs out" ticket. Like the FDC, Wine and his following were targeted with arrests and disappearances, yet Wine's popularity possibly opens the door to a younger generation of opposition voters (although Museveni has removed presidential age limits and appears willing to contest future elections or position his family to take over the NRM leadership).

Given Uganda's violent postindependence history, the transition to multipartyism is impressive; however, scholars question the degree to which elections are truly competitive and representative given NRM supremacy and opposition suppression (Tripp 2010; EIU 2021). Freedom House labels the country "not free" (Repucci and Slipowitz 2021), and because there has been no executive alternation it is classified as an electoral autocracy (Alizada et al. 2021). Ugandans nonetheless support democracy: in the first Afrobarometer (2000), 80 percent preferred democracy over other alternatives, and in the 2017 survey, 81 percent registered approval for democracy.

Turnout has been impressive before and after the transition to multipartyism (Table C.1). In 1996, turnout was 73 percent; in 2001 and 2006, 70 percent. It dipped to 59 percent in 2011, increased to 68 percent in 2016, and was 59 percent in 2021.

3.3.2 Psychic and Material Incentives

Given NRM dominance and little expectation of alternation, why do a majority of Ugandans bother casting ballots? Ethno-regional mobilization – particularly divisions between Northern and non-Northern groups – has been central to Uganda's political history and could influence politicians' organizational strategies and voters' sentiments. Table C.2 details the ethnic distribution. The Baganda (residing near the capital Kampala) are a plurality and comprise under 20 percent of the population. Immediately after independence, national governance required balancing associations between and among tribes, and traditional kingdoms. Buganda was largely autonomous and other kingdoms semi-autonomous, sparking anti-Baganda resentment. The Baganda are like Ghana's Ashanti and Kenya's Kikuyu in that they were most affected by the British colonial imprint, but they are unlike them in that their political power was long neutralized by other groups, primarily from the North. Under Obote and Amin (both Northerners), politics often centered around promoting their regional interests while demoting Buganda. Museveni, who hails from the Western region and the Bahima ethnic group (a Banyankole subtribe; Besigye belongs to the related Bahororo) – explicitly pitched NRM as a nationwide movement. But divisions between the North and other regions persisted from the 1990s to 2000s as the government fought the Lord's Resistance Army (LRA), a primarily Northern and ethnic Acholi inspired insurgent group.

At the same time, the impact of regional and ethnic identities on electoral politics is constrained by the reality that parties today are not primarily associated with specific groups or areas. Museveni has pragmatically drawn support from numerous bases beyond his Bahima/Banyankole (Golooba-Mutebi and Hickey 2016) and managed to improve his standing in the North in recent elections. Table C.2 (column 2) shows Museveni's voter support by respondent ethnicity in our 2011 exit poll. He gained majorities from all groups except the Baganda and Acholi; his Banyankole supported him at 73 percent, similar levels to other groups. His cross-regional support is also strong in our exit poll (Table C.3), where he obtained 72 percent support in his Western home, 60 percent in the Northern region, and managed 54 percent in Central, which includes Kampala. Besigye was popular primarily in urban centers and among more educated Ugandans, as was Wine, an ethnic Baganda from Kampala, who also appealed to the youth vote by burnishing reformist credentials (although Museveni portrayed him as a Baganda chauvinist).

In our 2011 pre-election survey, 12 percent of respondents reported feeling more strongly attached to their ethnic group relative to their national identity (Table C.5; 45 percent felt equally). Turnout does not correlate strongly with region (Table C.4); even though turnout was highest in Western (75%), it was similarly robust in Eastern (71%), Central (65%), and Northern (66%) regions. Ethnic attachments may serve at best as a mild motivation for turnout.

What about material incentives? Vote-buying is illegal and expensive but potentially pervasive.[22] Findings from the 2019 Afrobarometer suggest expectations of contingent exchanges are somewhat usual while understood to be illegal: 56 percent replied that it is wrong and punishable for candidates or political party officials to offer money in return for a vote, while 27 percent considered it wrong but understandable. 14 percent replied that it is not wrong at all (Kakumba 2020), reflected in Gulu, where "Charges of bribery, of the distribution of salt, of the dispensing of 'Kasese' (locally distilled gin) and meat to influence would-be voters were heard and existed in plenty in the news media" (Gingyera-Pinyewa and Obong-Oula 2003: 71). Museveni uses government appointments, bureaucratic employment, and government contracting as a form of patronage to NRM backers and members of the security services, and to woo local political bosses in hopes of swaying voters in their area. It is not uncommon for Ugandans to "eat widely but vote wisely" (accept gifts and then vote with their conscience), although voters admit to feeling compelled to reciprocate gifts/bribes with their ballot (Blattman et al. 2019).

Cash handouts may also only have a marginal effect on voting behavior or fail to persuade people. Out of exit poll respondents, 29 percent believed it was "very" or "somewhat" important that candidates reward supporters with gifts or money; however, when asked why they did not receive more services from the central government, 48 percent of our pre-election survey respondents blamed "misuse of funds" (Table C.5), revealing displeasure at what citizens perceive as government corruption. Guardado and Wantchekon (2018) note that "some previously targeted individuals shifted their allegiance from [the NRM] to FDC, consistent with the idea that handouts do not 'purchase' permanent

---

[22] Annual GDP per capita in 2011 was USD 832.

loyalty to a party" (18), and Blattman and colleagues (2018) show recipients of the Youth Opportunities Program, designed by the NRM, are no more likely to support the ruling party in elections.

Violence has occurred before, during, and after elections – less than in Kenya but more than in Ghana. Besigye and his FDC supporters were routinely harassed from 2006 to 2016, as was Wine in 2021, when reports documented extensive use of teargas, beatings, and the use of live bullets against his followers (Human Rights Watch 2021). Threats add to the impact of the country's use of community police – so-called "crime preventers" – during election periods, when the widespread presence of over 1,000,000 affiliated youth has been used to "destabilize and co-opt" the opposition (Tapscott 2016: 694) The LRA was also active in the early 2000s. Although having mostly been defeated by 2011, 22 percent of our pre-election respondents that year reported that their area had experienced attacks from insurgents since 2006. When asked about the likelihood of violence in their area on the upcoming election day, 33 percent of respondents believed it to be "very" or "somewhat" likely. A full 64 percent of voters registered at least some fear of "becoming a victim of political intimidation or violence" during election campaigns (Afrobarometer Round 5). Many nonetheless voted.

3.3.3 Social Sanctioning

Next, we examine why Ugandans might vote despite knowing the costs, and even when they may have little desire to, given communal pressure and opportunities for turnout verification.

Similar to trends across African countries revealed in surveys, Ugandans strongly attribute the provision of services – from roads to schools to clinics – to the government, and citizens are sensitive to government actions affecting community welfare. Subsequent regimes have taken sometimes aggressive, if also mixed, actions to address economic problems. Obote was a self-declared but ultimately unsuccessful developmentalist, while Amin's rule decimated the country. But after Museveni took over, he focused first on establishing order and then on economic policy and public goods provision, which has helped him to remain popular (Golooba-Mutebi and Hickey 2016).

Under the NRM, community signaling of support to the national government is important in order to receive local services. Museveni uses state resources to recruit NRM backing and reward his loyalists with lucrative positions, buy off opponents, and fund his clientelist network. For voters, he employs populist strategies to secure performance-based loyalty (e.g., "poverty tours") that involve listening to local concerns and distributing public goods (Bukenya and Hickey 2019). Universal Primary Education was a popular policy and campaign issue in 1996, when Museveni promised to abolish school fees (Stasavage 2005). Despite persistent tensions between the North and central government, Museveni increased cross-regional appeal to Northern constituents, who credit him with ending the LRA insurgency and rebuilding infrastructure. Out of 2011 exit poll respondents, 65 percent (and 63% of Northerners) strongly approved of the government's handling of the recovery in the North.

Ugandans likely perceive pressure to vote from community members. Even though Uganda is an electoral autocracy, 84 percent of Afrobarometer Round 6 respondents replied that a good citizen is someone who "always" votes, while 14 percent said "only if they choose." Election days are vibrant and boisterous, especially in rural areas and urban slums. In our pre-election survey, 63 percent responded that their neighbors would know whether or not they had turned out to vote (Table C.5), possibly contributing to perceptions of social pressure.

Because Ugandan politics are dominated by a single party and no single ethnic group has a majority, local communities are a key axis along which political mobilization occurs. This is also due in part to an emphasis on grass-roots consensus decision-making within LCs, which radiate out of concentric levels from the neighborhood to town and district. These local dynamics make many races more competitive than they might otherwise appear, both in terms of signaling support for or opposition to the NRM, and in terms of competition for NRM backing.

Accordingly, local candidates are well known to their constituents. In Cheeseman, Lynch, and Willis's (2021) survey, 74 percent of Ugandans could correctly name their MP, and the authors argue that "[e]lectoral experience in Uganda has therefore come to encourage a popular focus on parliamentary and local government elections as a way to make claims on local representatives, who serve as emissaries to an executive presidency that is effectively beyond the power of the ballot" (75). Barkan (1997) notes that for rural and even a significant number of urban voters, the "local community is the natural constituency or interest for which one seeks political representation" (13), which he attributes to shared interests resulting from similar economic (as opposed to ethnic) livelihoods tied to residential location (in line with our Section 2.3.3 discussion).

Gender and household characteristics also matter for galvanizing participation. From female recruitment into the NRA to the expansion of LCs, Museveni has explicitly enlisted women's support. Although women still face discrimination in public life in many ways, they turn out in large numbers (and vote for Museveni at a higher rate than men). Female candidates also frequently obtain

LC seats. "Museveni garnered support as a result of his government's projection of gender issues as a key policy in its development programs. Museveni is seen by most women as having 'liberated' them by way of bringing them into the political limelight at local level in LCs and national level as ministers" (Makara 2003a: 21). In a survey from urban Kampala (Appendix C), when asked if they go to the polls alone or in a group, 33 percent of respondents reported that they went to vote with family and friends, providing further evidence that voting is – purposely or incidentally – communal and public.

A variety of other actors facilitate collective action and forge ties with formal institutions, including parties. Unlike the opposition, the NRM can harness state resources and the security services to drive turnout in their enclaves, not just for Museveni but also for his allies and local candidates. On the morning of the 2011 election, Ugandans (and both authors) received "robo-calls" with a prerecorded message from Museveni "reminding" everyone to vote. Figure C.2 shows security agents watching a station open in urban Kampala. In Kampala, we also noticed routine police and military patrols in strong FDC neighborhoods, which tracks with the government's use of intimidation tactics more broadly. Regardless of these disadvantages, electoral races for parliamentary positions remain lively affairs, even for non-NRM candidates, particularly in regions with locally strong mobilization, such as among the Acholi and Baganda.

Traditional authorities are important to political life in Uganda. Kingdoms were one of the key divisions following independence, and traditional leaders are still central figures, particularly in rural areas where some were pivotal in resisting colonial rule and managing land rights. When asked if they "approve or disapprove of the government's handling of the role of traditional leaders," 20 percent of our exit poll respondents strongly approved and 28 percent approved, implying that many see layered authority as an important aspect of politics. Ugandans are also very religious, with 84 percent Christian and 14 percent Muslim; both Museveni and opposition figures routinely seek religious leaders' endorsements, and church groups rally turnout and serve as election observers.

Candidates have relied heavily on additional brokers to garner electoral backing. LC members often position themselves as important linkages between the parties and area residents. "LC II executives are highly knowledgeable of people who live in their localities and know the political leanings of their village mates" (Byarugaba 2003: 95). The strength of brokers is evidenced by a nationwide study during 2016 showing that interventions focused on reducing the strength of reciprocity between brokers and voters can increase competitiveness by favoring disadvantaged challengers (Blattman et al. 2019).

Community observation of turnout decisions and sanctioning are possible, even easy. "Sunshine" laws mean all voting and counting must occur outside when possible (Presidential Elections Act of 2005 [ULII 2005]). Most polling stations are in open-air locations: fields, school yards, and church grounds. Voting is time-consuming and requires long – sometimes all-day – queuing. Our observations throughout Kampala saw groups of voters waiting early in the morning for the polls to open, with steady streams throughout the day. It is easy to be seen (Figures C.1–C.2).

While analysts believe Museveni would likely win (or come close) in a fair vote, and relatively few (10%) Ugandans had the secrecy of their ballots compromised as reported in our exit poll, there are frequent irregularities, including missing ballot papers, illegally opened ballot boxes, and within the aggregation process (Callen et al. 2016). Museveni deploys NRM apparatchiks to (seem to) observe and record who votes (Makara 2003b); to a lesser degree, the FDC and Wine have also deployed agents to monitor voting and perform parallel vote tabulations. The polling station vote count is also famously a community affair. Voter education materials include a reminder that after their vote is cast, voters may come back to the station to watch the count and expect the results to be announced immediately (Government of Uganda n.d.), reflected in a tally that is posted on a wall, door, or tree. When we observed in Kawempe South Constituency (Kampala), we witnessed large gatherings of residents and neighbors socializing while waiting for election officials to prepare for the count. Once the count started, they cheered as election officials counted a ballot for their favored candidate and booed when ballots were tallied for their opponent (Figure C.3).

Uganda uses indelible ink to mark voters' fingers (Figure C.4). While putatively intended to prevent double-voting, Ferree and colleagues (2020) document its use in Uganda to make visible a person's turnout decision for several days. Their postelection survey finds 18 percent of respondents say the use of visible ink made them more likely to vote. "In Kamuli voting area, it was reported that LC official after voting went house to house in the village demanding to know whether people had finished voting especially those homes which were known to support Museveni" (Makara 2003b: 130).

3.3.4 Quantitative Analysis

We summarize our quantitative analyses using a pre-election survey from 2011 (described in Appendix C). In Table C.6 we report differences in means. Among those reporting their neighbors know whether they voted, intent to turn out was 91 percent; but among those who reported their neighbors would not know whether they voted, turnout declined to 84 percent (p<0.01). We find no significant difference in means across ethnic identifiers, a proxy for vote-buying, or those who expect violence. In multivariate tests (Table C.7), we observe a strong, positive association between our measure of social sanctioning, increasing turnout by between about four to five points (p<0.01), and no consistent, statistically significant relationships between ethnic identifiers, vote-buying, or violence (results remain robust to inclusion of additional socio-demographic and political controls).

As in Ghana and Kenya, so too in Uganda: some of the turnout puzzle appears resolved by considering social sanctioning. NRM dominance in Ugandan elections does not make them dull affairs: quite the opposite – like Ghanaians and Kenyans, Ugandans participate in strong numbers.

3.4 Conclusion

Section 3 results support our first two hypotheses, demonstrating both the effects of social sanctioning on turnout and its relative importance compared to other important psychic and material drivers. Across party systems in three third-wave African countries, we find consistent evidence of a broad belief among citizens that voting is important for the community and operates beyond the mobilizing role of expressive ethnic voting, vote-buying, and often violence. We document an awareness that people within the community monitor and sanction voting, and election administration makes the act of voting highly visible. What about participation in a much weaker, more unstable, and more violent democracy?

4 Testing the Theory in a Fragile State: Afghanistan

We turn to electoral participation in a fragile state, Afghanistan. Such states often result from the reconfiguration of political authority after violent regime change, state collapse, or foreign intervention. They differ from the modal developing country in that they are more conflict-prone, aid-dependent, and lack bureaucratic capacity. Since the Cold War, fragile states have arisen following military invasion (e.g., Iraq, Afghanistan), the Arab Spring (e.g., Yemen, Libya), and internationally supported postwar reconstruction (e.g., Sierra Leone, South Sudan). Donors and civil society activists frequently advocate and sponsor electoral assistance in fragile states to promote peace and establish formal linkages of service provision and political accountability between citizens and newly elected representatives. Understandably, participation requires overcoming significant hurdles given unstable political order. These contexts therefore present not only the highest bar for turnout, but also allow us to examine participation precisely where policy interventions have been applied to strengthen democratization in the weakest of institutional settings.

After the Taliban regime's 2001 overthrow by the United States and coalition allies, the international community worked with Afghans from all walks of life to reconstitute a civilian government, and subsequent aid directed billions of dollars for democracy promotion. But most noteworthy were Afghan voters themselves. Millions braved long lines – often in sweltering heat amid insurgent threats – in every national election starting in 2004, when turnout reached nearly 80 percent. Afghans participated in this democratic experiment despite widespread poverty, limited experience with functioning government institutions, and an absence of mobilizing parties. While turnout was robust through subsequent presidential (2009, 2014) and parliamentary (2010) elections, it began to decline by the last legislative (2018) and executive (2019) contests before the Taliban regained government control during the 2021 US withdrawal, effectively ending democracy for the foreseeable future. Given the challenges they faced – considerably more than Ghanaians, Kenyans, and Ugandans – why did so many Afghans vote?

In this section, we employ qualitative and quantitative data from Afghanistan, and field experience witnessing elections there. As in Section 3, we review Afghanistan's political development, electoral setting, and marshal descriptive evidence to assess the presence of psychic and material motivations, before turning to aspects of social sanctioning. We then present a research design to more systematically test our hypotheses from a nationwide survey conducted during 2010's parliamentary elections. Beyond applying our theory in another regional and institutional context, this endeavor provided several empirical advantages: it allowed innovation in measures of social sanctioning and its components, and a test of our third hypothesis on how trust and social capital condition sanctioning in ongoing conflict environments. It also permitted investigation in a country with no party system to speak of, and without concurrent presidential and legislative elections. The case carries implications for policies advocating democratization in unstable countries that impact regional and international security, including why recent declining turnout may have presaged democracy's collapse, a subject on which this section concludes.

4.1 Setting

Afghanistan's modern history has witnessed consolidation of territory and governing institutions from the eighteenth century to the present, with recent cycles of conflict, Taliban rule, democratization, and backsliding.

Ahmad Shah of the Durrani tribal line established an Afghan Kingdom in 1747 based in southern Kandahar, uniting the Durrani with other Pashtun tribes and ethnic Uzbeks, Tajiks, Hazaras, and others. Shah's kingdom encompassed Afghanistan's current boundaries and large swaths of what would become British India. His descendants relocated the capital north to Kabul, which Britain occupied to control as a buffer zone between czarist Russia and India during the First Anglo-Afghan War (1839–42). After the British retreated following the Second Anglo-Afghan War (1878–80), they officially imposed the Durand Line in 1893, demarcating the boundary with India and effectively dividing the previously consolidated Pashtun confederation between Afghanistan and present-day Pakistan.

With few interruptions, Pashtun royals continued to rule Afghanistan. Abdur Rahman Khan, the so-called Iron Amir, centralized political authority during his reign (1880–1901), and following the Third Anglo-Afghan War Britain recognized the country's independence (1919). Amanullah Khan worked to improve governance by writing a constitution, but in 1929 he was overthrown by Habibullah Kalakani, a Tajik, himself quickly ousted by rebels who restored Pashtun hegemony under Muhammad Nadir Shah. Nadir Shah continued Amanullah's modernizing direction but was assassinated in 1933. His son, Muhammad Zahir Shah – then only nineteen – nominally ruled while his powerful relatives, including cousin Daoud Khan, exerted control as regents.

In 1964, Zahir Shah convened a national *loya jirga* (grand council), which undertook democratic reforms and adopted a republican constitution. The constitution empaneled a National Assembly, including a lower house (Wolesi Jirga) elected from each province, and an independent judiciary, and kept the existing king as head of state. Parliamentary elections took place in 1965 and 1969. Zahir Shah proved popular as Afghanistan's economy performed well during the 1960s. Rural areas lagged in development compared to Kabul and regional capitals, but the national government allowed peripheral provinces relative autonomy.

As economic progress began to slow in the 1970s, opposition to Zahir Shah grew. A pro-Soviet communist alliance in Kabul intensified, while Islamist sentiments fomented in rural areas. With tensions among these camps rising, Daoud Khan, backed by the armed forces, overthrew Zahir Shah in 1973. Though Daoud initially had soft support from the United States, he increasingly looked to the Soviet Union to shore up his government. However, the communist wing in Kabul was rife with divisions between hardliners and moderates, like Daoud, who was assassinated in 1978. He was replaced by Nur Mohammed Taraki, a popular leftist reformer who established the Democratic Republic of Afghanistan, but Taraki was soon outflanked and overthrown by a more avowedly pro-Soviet faction, which galvanized sectarian fighting in Kabul. This sparked rebellion by anticommunist groups in many provinces.

To bolster their floundering Cold War ally, the Soviet Union invaded in 1979. Challenges to the Soviets and their puppet regime in Kabul grew as Islamist *mujahideen* insurgents – with support from the United States, Pakistan, and Saudi Arabia – fought against the government and Soviet troops, precipitating the latter's ignominious 1989 withdrawal. After the Soviet Union's own collapse, a communist government under Mohammad Najibullah held on until 1992, after which mujahideen fighters battled for control in Kabul – like the powerful Uzbek warlord Abdul Rashid Dostum, the (mostly Tajik) Northern Alliance under Ahmad Shah Massoud's command, and (Pashtun) Gulbuddin Hekmatyar's *Hezb-e-Islami*. Instability reigned in other cities and rural districts.

Amid this chaos, the Taliban, a primarily Pashtun group, recruited membership throughout the south (with support from Pakistani intelligence services) and captured Kandahar in 1994; by 1996, they controlled Kabul and remaining provinces, sending mujahideen forces to retreat to their rural redoubts (Massoud's Northern Alliance army held in the Panjshir Valley). The Taliban were the first regime in decades to establish anything like a monopoly on political authority, but instead of rebuilding institutional capacity they maintained law and order through repressive tactics and appeals to strict religious governance using brute force.

By 2001, the country had all but collapsed. Basic human welfare indicators of development placed Afghanistan at the global bottom, reversing its trajectory from before the 1970s. In the provinces, communities relied for protection and services on self-help or locally powerful patrons – warlords like Massoud and Dostum. The Taliban were an international pariah, held afloat by Pakistan but mostly ignored by the international community. A barely functioning government needing financing created an environment well-suited to host training camps for al-Qaeda terrorists. Under Osama bin Laden's direction, al-Qaeda suicide bombers murdered Massoud in Panjshir two days before, and in anticipation of, the September 11th attacks. The United States then invaded Afghanistan to overthrow the Taliban and hunt al-Qaeda, first by CIA-backed support to the Northern Alliance (now led by Mohammad Fahim after Massoud's death) and then US and coalition ground forces in October 2001. The Taliban and al-Qaeda retreated, many to eastern or southern Afghanistan, or Pakistan.

After the Taliban's ouster, international partners worked with stakeholders (excluding the Taliban), mediated by the UN, to create a transitional government via a series of loya jirgas in the Bonn Process (2001–5). The UN tasked partners with state-building and designing new governance institutions. Hamid Karzai, an influential Pashtun from a powerful Kandahari family, was appointed head of a transitional administration in late 2001. In 2002, an emergency loya jirga met with thousands of representatives from all over Afghanistan. Relying much on the design of the 1964 constitution, this council affirmed Karzai as president. A subsequent constitutional loya jirga shaped the electoral laws, and in October 2004 Afghans went to the polls to elect their head of state for the first time. Karzai won with 55 percent. A reconstituted popularly elected parliament, Wolesi Jirga, held elections a year later in September 2005, concluding the Bonn Process.

Despite attacks from a resurgent Taliban and frequent delays and rigging allegations, elections were core to Afghanistan's post-Taliban democratization. After the landmark 2004 race, presidential elections took place in 2009, when Karzai was re-elected. In 2014, Ashraf Ghani, a Pashtun and Karzai's former finance minister, won the presidency to succeed Karzai, and Ghani was re-elected in 2019 (with 50.6%). Abdullah Abdullah, a powerful Tajik who had served alongside Massoud and then as Karzai's foreign minister, was Karzai's main challenger in 2009 and in both elections against Ghani.[23] After 2005, Wolesi Jirga elections were held in 2010 and, following delays, in 2018. During the final US troop withdrawal in 2021, the Taliban retook Kabul and nearly all provinces, bringing the civilian government to an end, with Ghani fleeing into exile.

In its democratization period, Afghanistan had an uncommon electoral system and no party system. Presidential and parliamentary elections were not concurrent. Presidential races were decided with a 50 percent +1 majority two-round runoff like our African cases, but members of the Wolesi Jirga were elected in thirty-four multi-member province-wide districts through a single nontransferable vote (SNTV). SNTV mixes plurality rules with multiple seat allocations; aspirants ran at large in provinces with a first-past-the-post allocation of votes to seats. With 249 total seats up for grabs, 2,502 candidates contested in 2010. Kabul had the highest seat share (33) and Nimroz, Nuristan, and Panjshir the lowest (2). With SNTV, the thirty-three highest vote-getters in Kabul would obtain seats, as would the two highest in Nimroz, Nuristan, and Panjshir. Afghanistan also lacked formal parties. Parties have historically been viewed with suspicion and associated with past ideological and sectarian battles, and Karzai issued a decree forbidding parties. In 2010, fewer than 13 percent of parliamentary aspirants were officially aligned; the rest contested as independents.

Given the number of contestants for multiple seats and without party coordination, many parliamentary candidates ran and only a small proportion won due to small marginal vote share increases. Although Kabul had thirty-three

---

[23] In these races, Abdullah contested certified results. In 2009, he boycotted a runoff, and after losing the 2014 runoff to Ghani, Ghani appointed Abdullah to a ministerial "chief executive" post.

seats, over 400 individuals contested in 2005, 664 in 2010, and about 800 in 2018. In 2010, Panjshir and Nimroz only had two seats but yielded 12 and 13 candidates, respectively; Ghor, with the median six seats, had 39 aspirants. This presented lumpy dispersions of vote shares across many candidates. In 2010, only 37 percent of all votes went to winning candidates; in Kabul, nearly 70 percent of the vote went to losing candidates, as did a little more than half in Panjshir, effectively "wasting" these ballots. The top vote-getter in Kabul received 16,233 votes, only 3.6 percent of the total; in Kandahar, the first ranked winner received 7.5 percent. The number of votes that separated the final winning candidate, say that ranked thirty-third in Kabul, from the highest losing candidate, that ranked thirty-fourth, was often small: the lowest Kabul winner won 1,119 votes (0.3% of the total) beating the highest losing candidate by just eight ballots.

Despite various challenges, the newness of democratic institutions excited millions of Afghans to mobilize to vote in transitional elections. Afghan-born US Ambassador Zalmay Khalilzad (2016) recounts observing election day in 2004:

> [T]urnout took real courage. No one knew whether the Taliban would disrupt the voting with violence. There were many stories of Afghans writing their will or taking the equivalent of last rites in case they were killed at the polling stations ... Afghans were full of wonder that an election was actually happening .... One voter captured the national mood on Election Day: "Finally, we are human again." (212)

Because Taliban insurgents threatened elections and the regime faced a host of governance challenges, Freedom House coded Afghanistan's democracy as "not free." Observers were skeptical about democracy's trajectory, especially after 2014. The timing of our empirical exercise (2010) may have come at a moment when Afghans, previously supportive of the civilian government, had started to register concern for a lack of progress on strengthening institutions and bureaucratic capacity. In a pre-election survey, we asked about preferences for democracy: 50 percent replied that democracy is preferable to any other form of government, 21 percent that in some circumstances a nondemocratic government may be preferred, and 23 percent said regime did not matter. The Taliban have historically rejected democracy and understood voter participation harmed them politically as it signaled compliance with the government. They appear unwilling to allow elections as of writing.

Actual turnout *rates* are hard to estimate; the country lacked a recent census and accurate voter registry. However, we preview likely figures based on total ballots cast. Projections for 2004 were about 8.1 million, or 80 percent of voters, on the assumption that 10.5–11 million could be registered. In 2005, roughly 6.4 million people voted for parliament. About 4.5 million turned out in 2009, a decline that potentially signaled dissatisfaction with Karzai's government. The best estimates for 2010, the election during our data gathering, place turnout between 5–6 million voters (50–70%), with variation due to location (Appendix D). Although the numbers are debated, in 2014 the election commission reported presidential turnout was 6.6 million for the first round and 7.9 million for the runoff (Kraemer 2014). The most recent contests saw significantly reduced rates, however, with only 2 million votes in the 2018 parliamentary elections and 1.1 million in the 2019 presidential elections (Al-Jazeera 2019).

4.2 Psychic and Material Incentives

While never universal, Afghanistan experienced impressive participation considering the constraints voters faced. Depending on a reader's prior assumptions, the application of psychic and material incentives may be more or less obvious in predicting turnout in Afghanistan compared to Ghana, Kenya, and Uganda. We provide descriptive evidence interrogating these possibilities.

A psychic duty to vote could certainly arise from the mobilizing power of ethnicity, long a divisive axis and source of local and national conflict. The government has not published a recent census yet estimates put the Pashtun as a plurality (42%), with Tajiks (27%), Uzbeks (9%), and Hazaras (9%) the other largest groups. None comprises a nationwide majority, but each enjoys local province and district majorities. Representatives of ethnic groups historically marginalized by Pashtuns have long advocated for federalism and decentralization; although it is also the case that Tajiks, Uzbeks, and Hazaras, who were once regional warlords or backed the Northern Alliance, served in post-Taliban administrations,[24] won parliamentary seats, and were appointed to provincial offices. Decades of sectarian strife could have strengthened ethnic ties, and Afghans may voice political preferences through expressions of ethnic solidarity, particularly absent formal political parties.

There are also reasons to question the extent of ethnicity's mobilizing power. Afghans have deep feelings of, and pride in, their national identity. Assertions of nationalism have often been perceived as resentment toward outsiders, understandable considering Afghanistan's history of invasion, but nationalism can also cut against ethnic chauvinism. In our survey, 6 percent expressed more

---

[24] These include Abdullah (mixed Tajik/Pashtun), Karzai's former foreign minister and presidential aspirant; Fahim (Tajik), Karzai's vice president; and Dostum (Uzbek), Ghani's vice president.

closeness to their ethnic group, while approximately 70 percent expressed more closeness to their national identity (22% tied, Table D.1). Voter turnout revealed variation across and within ethnic enclaves, including for Pashtuns.

Participation is also potentially sensitive to material incentives. Afghanistan had some of the world's lowest development indicators and widespread poverty in 2001, which improved in the first decade after the US invasion, including life expectancy and school enrollment. But Afghans remained largely impoverished,[25] and increasingly so after 2016. In our pre-election survey, 60 percent of respondents thought it "very" or "somewhat" likely candidates would give money to people for votes. Anecdotally, allegations of vote-buying were abundant during campaigns. Not organized by established parties, efforts often operated locally. "One candidate in Kandahar is reported to have distributed tins of edible oil with his picture pasted to them" (Wilder 2005: 28). Linkages between various levels of government has historically meant that people have tried to use their access to gain bureaucratic employment, including for agencies or nongovernmental organizations that received lucrative aid contracts after 2001.

Simultaneously, political parties were effectively nonexistent, and many candidates lacked resources to pay many voters. The nature of weak governance meant that bureaucratic offices were often limited in supply. While material incentives were sometimes offered and received, there are reasons to believe they were neither universal nor deterministic of turnout.

Far more than in our African cases, Afghan voters routinely faced violent election periods. While 2004 and 2005 were relatively peaceful, insurgents significantly increased attacks in the lead-up to voting and on election days from 2009 onward, in orders of magnitude larger than terrorist attacks during non-election periods (Condra et al. 2018). Insurgents threatened candidates, election workers, polling stations, and specifically intimidated Pashtuns in hopes of deterring them from turning out – all to deprive the government of legitimacy. The need for the government to deploy additional police on streets and at polling stations may have further depressed turnout (Condra et al. 2019). Nevertheless, millions of Afghans managed to vote in every election after 2004.

4.3 Social Sanctioning

Although the political, social, and economic environment in which Afghans cast ballots is in many ways different from Ghana, Kenya, and Uganda, we suggest community expectations to vote and monitoring capacity of turnout nonetheless combined to generate perceptions of social sanctioning.

---

[25] 2010 GDP per capita was USD 543.

Afghans plausibly faced strong pressures to vote because citizens attributed service provision to the government. Despite patchy state-building after 2001, in our (2010) pre-election survey, when asked who was mainly responsible for delivering services in their neighborhood, most Afghans gave a response mentioning government: 39 percent said central government, 15 percent member of parliament, 23 percent provincial government, and 10 percent community development councils; only 11 percent said nongovernment sources, like religious or ethnic leaders. The Wolesi Jirga specifically played an important role legislating national matters and providing local public goods by individual members in their provinces. In the same survey, 60 percent of respondents said the opportunity to vote in parliamentary elections increases the quality of services in their neighborhood, 62 percent believed voting for the Wolesi Jirga increases the happiness of people living in their neighborhood, and 89 percent thought the Wolesi Jirga was very or somewhat important in helping to improve life in their neighborhood. 65 percent replied voting leads to improvements in the future, suggesting nascent, if imperfect, institutions were still viewed by many as important sources of service provision (although 30 percent said no matter how one votes things never change).

In our pre-election survey, 88 percent of respondents said it was "somewhat" or "very" important for everyone in their neighborhood to vote even if they did not like the candidates. Recall, the vote margin between the lowest winning and highest losing parliamentary aspirant was often narrow. As a result, candidates and the voters who supported them understood the importance of coordinating votes at the community level, or *manteqa*, "which loosely translates into 'area,' or cluster, of villages" (Murtazashvili 2016:175). In fact, so strong are residency ties that scholars like Barfield (2010) have argued they hold more sway than ethnic attachments – echoing Barkan's analysis from Africa – although most voters still resided in what were ethnically homogeneous polling precincts (true even in cities like Kabul where neighborhoods are divided by sect).

The electoral system benefited candidates who cultivated the personal vote and gained local support from relatives and area residents. Indeed, the realities of habitation pointed to the likelihood of concentrated vote shares for candidates by community, a dynamic which according to Coburn and Larson (2014), "continues to be based on a political logic that maximizes the resources a political group can secure" (126), and is demonstrated by this example of coordination for candidates for provincial council:

> With 11 different candidates from the area, there was the strong feeling that unless certain candidates were eliminated, they would split the community's vote and few, if any, would be elected …. A special shura meeting was

scheduled to address the issue ... the mullah of one of the large mosques in
Qara Bagh ... emphasize[d] that it was everyone's religious duty to vote and
that the people should form a coalition around one or two candidates .... Two
candidates from [Qara Bagh] had secured the necessary votes to join the
provincial council .... For many this was good news, since having two
representatives on the provincial council would hopefully bring more government resources to the district. (ibid.: 101–2)

Individual identities of viable candidates were well known to locals and the
absence of parties "put a premium on nonpolitical factors (such as name
recognition, ethnicity, region, and social standing)" (Barfield 2010: 301).[26] In
2010, 18 percent of our pre-election survey respondents reported a member of
their *qawm* (extended family/clan) was currently in parliament and 23 percent
knew of a qawm member running for parliament in 2010. Fully 30 percent
reported having a member of their qawm on their community development
councils, and 40 percent had qawm relatives in their provincial government.

[Q]aum membership and other social markers sometimes determine an individual's marriage choices, their rights and access to water and land, and, in
the case of representative governance, which individuals should have the
right to receive resources from their representatives .... These patterns and
forms of organizing are particularly important when we consider how both
candidates and local leaders have attempted to manipulate blocs of voters.
(Coburn and Larson 2014: 122–23)

In turn, "The success of candidates in portraying themselves as able to provide
the community with resources was a crucial aspect of almost all campaigns"
(ibid.: 118).

Hashmat Karzai's (Hamid's cousin) candidacy illustrates these electoral and
communal dynamics. In 2010, Hashmat campaigned for one of eleven seats in
Kandahar (against forty-nine others). The Karzai provenance derives from
Karz, a village outside of Kandahar City; many Karz inhabitants are related to
the Karzai family directly or by marriage. Hashmat was popular in Karz, and
residents had reason to support him:

Hashmat had plans to build a hospital and a new mosque in Karz .... Using
profits from his security company and from a hotel he ran for foreign
contractors outside Kandahar Airfield, Hashmat paid more than $2,000 to
repair all the broken windows in the Karz school after a bomb went off

---

[26] "The first network of support candidates turned to were those closest to home – family, friends
and neighbours. Beyond this inner circle the focus of candidate campaigns turned towards
winning the support of local influentials who could deliver blocs of votes based primarily on
religious or kinship grounds" (Wilder 2005: 17).

nearby. He claimed to have spent $70,000 of his own money to bring power lines to Karz, which had no steady source of electricity. (Partlow 2017: 289)

Karz School, the town's central polling precinct, had 775 votes cast, 695 of which went to Hashmat. The next highest candidate received 45 votes, and of the remaining contenders, only twenty received any votes (with an average of 1.75). Overall in Kandahar province, the highest winner netted 5,663 votes, the average number of votes for all candidates was 3,427, and the lowest winner received 627 votes (compared to the highest loser's 613). Hashmat's ability to receive such a high concentration and number of votes solely from his village put him in range to gain a seat.[27]

To enforce cooperation and advocate community participation in elections, additional layers of social networks and other actors facilitated collective action. Household dynamics matter to involvement in civic life. In more conservative (particularly Pashtun) areas, women rarely engage in public activities without a male or household escort. Wives are expected to defer to their husbands; youth are expected to defer to their elders. While voting was relatively more accessible for women in urban centers, in rural areas women often traveled to polling centers with their husbands and other household members. "In Paktya, strong tribal ties and an emphasis on kinship lead individuals to vote together as a family .... This in turn shapes campaigns, in which candidates try to secure entire blocs of votes" (Coburn and Larson 2014: 8).

During periods of turmoil, Afghans often rely on communal self-help for protection. Strong solidarity based on kinship, or *asabiya*, "bound[s] all members of a social group together ... the group interest trumps individual interest to such an extent that loyalty to the group supersedes everything else" (Barfield 2010: 58–59). We do not suggest that cultural practices necessarily overly determine electoral turnout, but rather that a variety of cultural institutions often interact with political institutions for understanding political behavior. Historically, while social networks have contributed to communal coordination to supply services, these informal sources of support have also worked directly and indirectly with formal government institutions; the type of service demanded is relevant – matters of justice and local disputes weighed toward traditional authorities, while infrastructure and other public goods leaned toward the government. In the post-Taliban period, community development councils, created by the National Solidarity Programme, allowed residents to vote on and oversee development projects in their villages.

---

[27] His victory was overturned after allegations that he bribed officials to inflate his vote elsewhere in Kandahar, votes he likely did not need given his strength in Karz.

Support from militia commanders has been another source of assistance. Warlords became important during the Soviet occupation and after, providing security and services for their communities. Many of those powerful actors then ran for, or were appointed to, public office (and gained popularity for their ability to deliver). Leaders in clans and religious institutions are also important for communicating norms and activating community efforts. If Afghans violate local strictures, family members, neighbors, and shuras (local traditional councils) may shun or sanction them. Given the importance of religion in Afghanistan – where 99 percent of the population is Muslim, mostly Sunni – religious leaders often mediate local legal and land disputes, broker peace between insurgents and local villages, and provided campaign resources around elections.

Other community leaders – *maliks*, or *qaryadars* – frequently played the role of vote broker. Such brokers served as intermediaries between elected leaders and communities and exerted mobilizing turnout pressure. Brokers would include village elders, school headmasters, and business owners (Coburn 2016).

> As one voter explained: "[The candidates] give money to elders or maliks
> for expenses and then the maliks go and buy meat, rice, and cold Pepsi.
> Then they prepare the food at home and invite people [to campaign events]."
> [C]ampaign workers, usually local elders, organized the gatherings and made
> speeches in support of the candidates. (Coburn and Larson 2014: 118–19)

Community brokers mattered precisely given "personalized parties" (Wilder 2005: 9), or candidates who ran with the resources at their disposal but who lacked financing from established parties:

> At the center of the relationship between candidates and (supposed) commu-
> nity voting blocs were a series of community leaders who claimed to be the
> political brokers that could control these blocs. ... [T]hey provided a focal
> point through which groups could reap the benefits of their collective strat-
> egies. (Coburn and Larson 2014: 126–27)

Elections were administered in such a way that permitted turnout monitoring, giving communities capacity to enforce expectations to vote. Election day was a public holiday with central locations (schools, mosques) serving as polling centers that made participation, by and large, observable. Gopal (2014) describes enthusiasm and visibility at a polling center in 2004: "By sunrise they arrived at the polling center, the main schoolhouse. ... [Voters] flashed toothy smiles and waved to UN photographers as they presented their registration cards and dipped a finger in purple ink to prevent multiple voting" (158). Individual balloting locations were typically rooms (streams) inside a school, and voters queued outside – as shown in Figure D.2. In 2010, average turnout per stream was 456 voters.[28] In Kabul the average geographic area covered by a polling center was 0.2 square miles. Figure D.2, Panels A–E are photos one author took of the process at various polling centers in Kabul, showing the public nature of voting.

Visibility allowed neighbors, political agents, and brokers to observe turnout. Coburn and Larson (2014) note, "Most of the main political leaders in town (or at least their representatives) spent a good deal of the day chatting in the bazaar next to the polling station, clearly observing who was voting and who was not" (109). Even though resource-constrained, candidates would deploy brokers and family members to rally voters and monitor the process in their areas of perceived support.

> Candidates hired agents to help campaign, provide voter education, observe the polls and monitor the counting process. As observed on election day, these agents often played an important role in assisting and, at times, pressuring voters to vote for their candidates ... [S]ome candidates reported that they could not afford any agents, and only had a few family and friends volunteering some help. (Wilder 2005: 28)

While aspects of voting were observable (particularly in lines outside of streams), security concerns required protections making monitoring more challenging compared to our African cases, especially in elections from 2009 onward – when insurgent threats and attacks increased, and the government improved force deployment to protect electoral sites and voters. Voters had to pass through security to gain entrance to polling centers' grounds, nearly always walled for protection, such as the perimeter around a school (Figure D.2). Nonetheless, when entering and exiting polling center grounds and when queuing, voters were still at least somewhat visible to the general public and other voters.

Observing the vote was possible in other ways, such as the aforementioned finger inking after casting a ballot (Figure D.4). Gopal (2014) recounts stories of voters being forced to pay fines after election day if they could not prove they voted: "'They charge you money for not voting, but it wasn't even my fault. I was traveling' .... Police officers were going from village to village announcing via loudspeaker that whoever hadn't voted had to pay a fine" (159). Inking was so iconic that members of the American Congress displayed purple fingers during George W. Bush's 2005 State of the Union address to signal support for his administration's policies in Afghanistan and Iraq. The Taliban also threatened to cut off inked fingers, especially Pashtuns. Although actual reports of

---

[28] While urban centers were on average somewhat larger, communities were more tightly clustered around them and it was logistically easier to vote in urban areas. On average they had higher turnout.

finger cutting were rare, polling staff reported some voters' requesting not to have their fingers marked. Polling center managers produced, and posted in a public spot, tallies showing the total votes cast for each candidate – typically the door to the school yard or wall outside of the classroom (Figure D.3). While tallies were accessible to any member of the public, candidates and their agents consulted them to assess their likely vote totals before the certified results were published, which took months. Tallies convey the degree of support in the area around the polling center, typically for a local son or daughter.[29]

4.4 Quantitative Analysis

To more systematically test our hypotheses, we use individual-level data from an original survey we designed and conducted during the September 2010 Wolesi Jirga elections. We surveyed 3,048 Afghans in 468 polling center catchment areas across nineteen (of thirty-four) provincial centers in all regions of the country two months after the election.[30] Our sampling procedure used polling centers as primary sampling units, reflecting our theoretical concerns regarding how people, when deciding whether to vote, perceive the likely behavior of their neighbors who would vote at the same place. As in Section 3, we do not suggest we can explain the turnout decisions of all voters; rather, we aim to compare and explore motivations driving individuals who might otherwise stay home to go to the polls.

Our dependent variable, *Turnout*, is based on whether a person reported they voted (yes=1). 67 percent of respondents reported voting, close to the IEC-announced rate of 62 percent (see Appendix D) and below the 76 percent who reported they intended to vote in our separate pre-election survey.[31] The explanatory variable *Social Sanctioning* derives from two survey measures: *Neighbors Expect*, a question asking respondents whether or not their neighbors expect them to vote even if undesirable candidates appear on the ballot, and *Neighbors Know*, a question asking whether respondents think other members of their community know whether or not they voted. We combine the measures to create *Social Sanctioning* (=1 if both *Neighbors Expect* and *Neighbors Know* are "yes").[32]

---

[29] "[I]t wasn't unusual for a village to report 90 percent support for a single candidate" (Gopal 2014: 261).

[30] Appendix D details the sampling strategy, measures, descriptive statistics, and robustness checks.

[31] The expected and realistic drop in reported turnout between survey waves gives additional confidence postelection over-reports of participation were not common (Table D.1).

[32] Appendix D discusses *Neighbors Expect* and *Neighbors Know*, showing off-diagonal categories are well-populated (Table D.2) and that the combination of the measures is not likely endogenous to reported voting behavior (Figure D.1 reports demographic correlates).

Social Sanctioning defined this way provides a good measure of perceptions of potential sanctioning. First, *Neighbors Expect* gauges the extent to which voters build expectations about the behavior of others with whom they will interact to succeed individually and collectively; it probes whether a respondent perceives others to have an expectation they vote, with 43 percent replying "yes." The question's wording explicitly imposes a negative cost on voting by specifying that the candidates are undesirable.[33] We asked *Neighbors Know* to capture whether there is a belief that the community can and will observe participation, with 47 percent reporting affirmatively, reflecting monitoring capacity is possible but not universal (due in part to security concerns). Overall, 28 percent of our sample perceived social sanctioning: their neighbors both expected them to vote and knew whether or not they had. This intersection highlights both social context and visibility of voting; their combination should have an increased effect on voting compared to their independent effects.[34]

We also tested the effects of psychic and material motivations, alongside a group of controls. *Ethnic Identifier*=1 for Afghans who feel closer to their ethnic than national identity. For material incentives, we probe respondents about the importance and expectation of candidates providing gifts to voters: *Vote-buying*=1 for positive responses. Analogous to the "violence" penalty in Table 1, *Community Violence*=1 if respondents report personal exposure to violence in the last five years.[35] We include a *Pashtun* dummy for respondents because of Taliban threats against Pashtun voters. An important turnout factor in a new democracy is a lack of knowledge of, or interest in, new institutions like parliament; accordingly, we probed their understanding with *Wolesi Jirga Importance*=1 if respondents reply that parliament is very or somewhat important in helping to improve life in their neighborhood, and *Services*=1 if respondents believe voting for the Wolesi Jirga provides the opportunities to improve local services in their neighborhood. We include dummies for whether a respondent is *Male*, *Literacy* (proxying education), and *Electricity* access (proxying income).

Table 2 presents ten linear probability estimations on likelihood of turnout, with robust standard errors in parentheses (clustered at the primary sampling unit, polling center). We examine whether and by how much social sanctioning increases the likelihood someone who would otherwise stay home votes, corresponding to cooperating to "participate" from Table 1. Models 1–4 test the theory's basic predictions with *Social Sanctioning*, *Ethnic Identifier*, and *Vote-buying*; Models 5–10 include controls.

---

[33] See footnote 15.

[34] Table D.6 assesses the component parts.

[35] Table D.5 also reports a robustness check to self-reported exposure to violence using administrative data on attacks.

Table 2 Linear probability model on voting (=1)

	(1)	(2)	(3)	(4)	(5)	(6)	(7)	(8)	(9)	(10)
Social Sanctioning	0.217***			0.216***	0.216***	0.217***	0.171***	0.190***	0.166***	0.166***
	(0.02)			(0.02)	(0.02)	(0.02)	(0.02)	(0.02)	(0.02)	(0.02)
Vote-buying		0.035		0.031	0.031	0.031	0.022	0.025	0.016	0.016
		(0.02)		(0.02)	(0.02)	(0.02)	(0.02)	(0.02)	(0.02)	(0.02)
Ethnic Identifier			−0.024	−0.028	−0.028	−0.028	0.005	0.007	0.009	0.009
			(0.04)	(0.04)	(0.04)	(0.04)	(0.04)	(0.04)	(0.04)	(0.04)
Community Violence					−0.002		−0.010	−0.001	−0.007	−0.008
					(0.02)		(0.02)	(0.02)	(0.02)	(0.02)
WJ Important						0.138***		0.205***	0.138***	0.138***
						(0.02)		(0.02)	(0.02)	(0.02)
Services							0.243***		0.211***	0.210***
							(0.02)		(0.02)	(0.02)
Male							0.070***	0.074***	0.069***	0.068***
							(0.02)	(0.02)	(0.02)	(0.02)
Literacy							0.105***	0.116***	0.098***	0.099***
							(0.02)	(0.02)	(0.02)	(0.02)

Electricity							0.036*	0.037*	0.034	0.035
							(0.02)	(0.02)	(0.02)	(0.02)
Pashtun						0.009	0.017			0.020
						(0.03)	(0.03)			(0.03)
Constant	0.608***	0.660***	0.670***	0.602***	0.603***	0.599***	0.353***	0.315***	0.277***	0.270***
	(0.01)	(0.01)	(0.01)	(0.01)	(0.01)	(0.01)	(0.02)	(0.03)	(0.03)	(0.03)
N	3048	3048	3048	3048	3048	3048	3048	3048	3048	3048
R^2	0.317	0.290	0.289	0.318	0.318	0.318	0.388	0.368	0.398	0.398

Standard errors in parentheses, clustered at PSU, $p<0.1$*, $p<0.05$**, $p<0.01$***

Social Sanctioning is positive, significant, and substantively large across all specifications. In Model 1, a voter who would otherwise stay home but perceives social sanctioning is nearly twenty-two points more likely to turn out than one who does not, an increase of 36 percent beyond baseline levels. The coefficients for *Ethnic Identifier* are negative and poorly estimated, and the effects of *Vote-buying* are poorly estimated and substantively small. *Wolesi Jirga Importance* and *Services* are consistently positive and significant. In Model 7, the *Services* coefficient shows respondents are about twenty-four points more likely to vote if they link parliament with local service provision, and in Model 8 respondents who think the Wolesi Jirga is important for improving life in the community were about twenty-one points more likely to vote than citizens who do not find it important. These two findings support both our assertion that voting is a mechanism to invest in collective goods and the interpretation that respondents were more likely to vote when they viewed participation as a consequential transaction between themselves and elected representatives with implications for communal welfare. Overall, these findings provide empirical support for our first and second hypotheses.[36]

Models 5–10 highlight other factors that affected voting likelihood. Voters who had experienced violence were only marginally less likely to vote. This may only partially proxy for actual violence on or near the election, but it may also reflect mixed results from other studies on violence exposure. Taliban intimidation certainly kept some voters at home, including Pashtuns, though on the whole they were no less likely to turn out. (*Pashtun* may therefore not be a good proxy for perceived violence or intimidation, or just reflect that Pashtuns were no less invested in elections.) *Male* and *Literate* voters were more likely to vote, while *Electricity* access had a small effect.[37]

Tests with survey data necessarily pose inferential threats regarding omitted variables, spurious or endogenous factors, and measurement bias. To address these concerns, in Appendix D we perform a series of extensive robustness checks employing supplementary data and tests from our survey, different models and measures, and additional administrative data. Those checks confirm our main results here. Although our data do not allow us to control perfectly for all unobserved factors or rule out definitively all possible confounding variables to isolate the precise causal effect of perceptions of social sanctioning on turnout, our tests, supported by these sensitivity analyses, produce results consistent with our theoretical intuition.

---

[36] Results remain robust to maximum likelihood estimation (Tables D.10 and D.11), province fixed effects (Table D.7), and an expanded definition of *Ethnic Identifier* (Table D.12).

[37] Whether respondents were born in the enumerated village or elsewhere also did no not affect turnout propensity.

4.5 Extending the Theory: Social Capital and Trust

According to our third hypothesis, differential levels of a community's social capital – measured by trust of one's neighbors – could strengthen or attenuate the effect of social sanctioning on turnout in an active conflict setting (Section 2.4). Indeed, many state-building institutions in Afghanistan, like the National Solidarity Programme, put rebuilding social capital in local communities as an explicit goal.

Table 3 presents identical specifications from Table 2, now separating the sample by reported trust in neighbors. Because people are likely playing cooperative games with varying social capital levels, we split the sample in Table 3 into one composed only of trusting (Models 4–6) and one of non-trusting (Models 1–3) individuals.[38]

Similar to the full sample, across all models *Social Sanctioning* is a significant, positive predictor of likelihood of voting, but its effect is larger among non-trusting individuals (Models 1–3) compared to trusting ones (Models 4–6), supporting hypothesis 3. For trusting individuals, *Social Sanctioning* improves turnout by about eighteen points (Model 6), while for individuals who do not trust their neighbors, sanctioning increases by twenty-two points (Model 3). For ease of interpretation, Figure 2 reports predicted probabilities on likelihood of voting from the same specification, first for the full sample (Table 2, Model 10), and then for the non-trusting (Table 3, Model 3) and trusting (Table 3, Model 6) subsamples, holding other variables at their means. In Figure 2, the effect of sanctioning is larger on the non-trusting subsample, increasing the likelihood of voting by roughly thirty-two points (from about 53 to 75%), compared to the trusting subsample that had a higher baseline level of voting (at 66%) that increased by eighteen points (to around 84%) with sanctioning. Although turnout remains high for both subsamples, when a person does not express trust for their neighbors the effect of social sanctioning is more potent than when people do trust their neighbors.

Table 3 demonstrates two additional interesting results. *Ethnic Identifier* remains insignificant, and *Vote-buying* is a significant and positive (although weak) predictor of voting but only within the non-trusting subset. With controls included these findings on *Vote-buying* fall just below conventional standards of statistical significance so we urge caution in interpreting them, however they potentially

---

[38] Trust Sample is: "How much do you trust your neighbors?" =1 if "very much" or "somewhat," 0 otherwise. Table D.8 replicates Table 3 with province-level fixed effects. Table D.9 re-estimates Table 3 with an interaction term for social sanctioning and trust on the full sample.

Table 3 Linear probability model of community trust on voting (=1)

	(1)	(2)	(3)	(4)	(5)	(6)
Social Sanctioning	0.267***	0.237***	0.220***	0.226***	0.181***	0.179***
	(0.04)	(0.04)	(0.04)	(0.03)	(0.03)	(0.03)
Vote-buying	0.077*	0.034	0.052	0.005	-0.006	-0.004
	(0.04)	(0.04)	(0.04)	(0.03)	(0.03)	(0.03)
Ethnic Identifier	-0.109	-0.097	-0.090	0.036	0.050	0.072
	(0.07)	(0.07)	(0.07)	(0.05)	(0.05)	(0.05)
Community Violence		0.006	0.005		0.008	0.006
		(0.04)	(0.04)		(0.03)	(0.03)
WJ Important		0.122***	0.119***		0.160***	0.148***
		(0.04)	(0.04)		(0.03)	(0.03)
Services		0.203***	0.190***		0.246***	0.233***
		(0.04)	(0.04)		(0.02)	(0.02)
Male			0.087***			0.032
			(0.03)			(0.02)
Literacy			0.072**			0.112***
			(0.03)			(0.02)

	(1)	(2)	(3)	(4)	(5)	(6)
Electricity			0.117***			-0.035
			(0.04)			(0.03)
Pashtun			0.032			0.016
			(0.06)			(0.04)
Constant	0.506***	0.339***	0.189***	0.647***	0.382***	0.325***
	(0.02)	(0.03)	(0.05)	(0.01)	(0.03)	(0.04)
Sample	Trust = 0	Trust = 0	Trust = 0	Trust = 1	Trust = 1	Trust = 1
N	1111	1111	1111	1937	1937	1937
R²	0.515	0.548	0.564	0.355	0.422	0.434

Standard errors in parentheses, clustered at PSU; p<0.1*, p<0.05**, p<0.01***

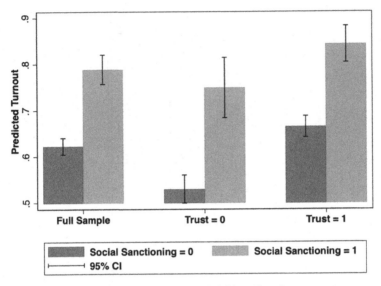

Figure 2 Predicted probability of voting

indicate that offering material incentives to individuals who lack trust may help to mobilize them.[39]

4.6 Conclusion

Turnout in Afghanistan indicates the plausibility of our predictions in a fragile state where voters faced some of the highest obstacles to participation in the world. But how do our results comport with the fall of the elected government in 2021, especially considering a dramatic decline in turnout in the 2018 and 2019 elections?

Social sanctioning hinges on citizens having expectations that their government provides public goods, which are linked to electoral participation. Our results from 2010 suggest that citizens attributed voting to the potential for actual progress in their lives. While we lack definitive evidence from more recent elections, we suspect an erosion of faith that voting makes a difference to improving services may explain some of the turnout decline. In an Asia Foundation survey from 2019, along with insecurity, voters cited "voting is not beneficial" as a prime reason to stay home, in contrast to our 2010 survey results where respondents expressed belief in the importance of voting because of the Wolesi Jirga's role in delivering services.

We consider a few alternative explanations. Perhaps political development and democratization *never* evolved to bring citizens close to the central

---

[39] Non-trusting individuals may also possibly have shorter time horizons, making more immediate, private (likely smaller) benefits important; or selective incentives could be more rampant and perhaps necessary for those in areas with lower levels of social capital.

government to sustain voting, or perhaps Afghans just preferred the Taliban. However, neither view can explain falling turnout, from 80 percent in 2004 to below 25 percent in 2019. Even if Afghans grew skeptical of the Karzai and Ghani governments and the Wolesi Jirga over time, they appear to have had reasons to participate at least through 2010. And life under the Taliban is demonstrably worse. Public opinion data in late 2021 compared responses from a survey conducted after the Taliban victory to the few years before; across nearly all dimensions, Afghans reported rapidly degrading conditions for themselves and communities (The Economist 2022).

Or perhaps community pressure and monitoring capacity for collective action simply declined for other reasons. Certainly, violence worsened after 2010, making election-day observation more dangerous; however, violence had already been increasing by 2009. Moreover, state-building, such as it was, always existed alongside other institutions and actors that mattered to Afghans' lives and maintaining local collective action. The failures of state-building did not manage to destroy communities' ability to coordinate; in fact, if evidence from other failed states, like Haiti, is suggestive, local collective action for survival can *increase* as state collapse grows worse (Jung and Cohen 2020).

Instead, pressure and monitoring are unlikely to be felt where communities no longer believe electoral participation aids collective action of the type our theory implies. We were not surprised to see turnout fall in Afghanistan and posit that the fault lies with the government's inability to fulfill the promises of the post-Taliban political arrangement. Our theory hinges on an implicit deal: in return for voting, communities expect life to get better – citizens see themselves in an iterated interaction with their representative government. Such a bargain has been largely upheld in Ghana, Kenya, and Uganda, but in fragile states it is harder to maintain. There, democracy may unravel as a result not only from the ravages of violent insurgency but also from the unmet demands of the voting public on the part of elected leaders.

5 Electoral Participation in Comparative Perspective

Why do so many people in emerging democracies continually participate in elections, and what might their voting behavior suggest about the trajectory of democracy globally?

This Element builds on rich literatures that demonstrate how individual psychic and material motivations have shaped our understanding about how citizens and politicians try to offset voting costs to inspire positive electoral mobilization. We ground our story of turnout in the social fabric of third-wave and fragile democracies, where voting involves not only an individual's personal utility but also the incentives they face to invest in collective goods for their community. Social pressure and the ability to monitor turnout can lead to tipping points generating widespread participation beyond what we might otherwise expect. Measuring perceptions through surveys and bolstered by other qualitative, survey, and administrative data, we paint a more holistic picture of electoral behavior and its social origins in the transitioning societies of the late twentieth and early twenty-first centuries.

We make several contributions to the study of political behavior, campaigns, and elections in emerging democracies – where inclusive governance and electoral participation are newer, less studied, and voting costlier, compared to established democracies. We account for how individual and community factors affect turnout and show our results hold despite different party systems with plurality electoral rules. Ghana's two-party system has seen competitive alternation and appears on the way to consolidation; Kenya's shifting political alliances make elections tense, occasionally violent, and outcomes hard to predict; Uganda's one-party dominance means many winners are known in advance. Nevertheless, these countries' elections recur, and turnout endures in remarkably consistent ways. Even in Afghanistan – the weakest of democracies with no parties to speak of – local pressure, reinforced by a host of formal and informal actors, inspired collective action for participation. Our theoretical mechanisms reflect features many developing countries share, and our data-gathering strategy is sufficiently generalizable to other settings.

Since electoral rules plausibly affect turnout rates by changing inducements for voters to coordinate action given how ballots are converted into seats, we expand briefly on the applicability of social sanctioning to nonplurality, proportional (PR) contexts. We believe the community and electoral features we identify likely generate expectations to vote and monitoring capacity in roughly equivalent ways (even if not levels) across electoral systems. Under PR, voter coordination is still necessary to advance community interests such that social sanctioning should remain strong (and perhaps be even stronger than under plurality rules) given that small increases in marginal vote shares correspond to seat shares. While direct evidence is beyond our scope, this is a fruitful future avenue.

This Element also advances insights on translating the role of social norms for voting from industrialized democracies. While that scholarship assumes widely held beliefs in a democratic duty to participate, it does not always reveal its source(s) or why some individuals appear to compel this duty on the part of others. We locate the origins of cooperative norms in emerging democracies not in democratic values per se (although citizens surveyed across developing regions support these values), but as a solution to local collective action in ways that benefit the community's welfare. We identify how community members and others can credibly enforce these norms through monitoring as facilitated by the way elections in many transitioning countries are conducted (e.g., the layout of polling stations, the practice of inking).

Last, we consider what our results suggest about the opportunities and challenges policymakers and citizens face in strengthening democratic institutions in light of recent, but growing, concerns of global democratic backsliding (Haggard and Kaufman 2021). Such concerns are legitimate responses to events like the Trump-inspired Capitol Insurrection, the increasingly authoritarian pulse of Viktor Orbán's behavior in Hungary, and Recep Tayyip Erdoğan's consolidation of power in Turkey. Moreover, in third-wave and fragile democracies, donors have spent significant resources on electoral assistance precisely to diffuse democracy worldwide, only to see many of those efforts undermined by various problems that have stalled the prospects for consolidation in many cases. Although frequently overlooked when others reflect on global patterns, voters from these countries might provide insights when fears of backsliding are cast in comparative perspective.

From classical Rome to modern-day Iraq, consolidation and legitimation of political order requires strong institutions. Electoral participation is a key signal of citizens' consent; electoral processes allow communities to express demands of delegates and foster accountable leaders. Institutions that bend toward representation of, and accountability by, the body politic are normatively preferable to those that constrain participation and undermine accountability. Yet elections also matter empirically in the actions they inspire and what they deliver. Cases like Afghanistan, or even Kenya and Uganda, seemingly question this democratic ideal type given how recent elections have played out. They perhaps suggest citizens either do not "get" what elections are supposed to be about or are unable to transform mobilization into improved governance. Observers then claim that the quality of democracy is in retreat because voters are apparently willing to abandon democratic principles – possibly due to their ethnic affinity, susceptibility to bribery, or propensity for violence. For their part, elected officials are cast as too corrupt, autocratic, or weak to govern in ways that support citizens' welfare.

Certainly, elections in transitioning societies often leave much to be desired. Normative commitments to democracy should not obfuscate the reality that elections sometimes appear to do more harm than good. At the same time, a too skeptical viewpoint could obscure the importance of elections even when they are far from perfect. Here, our results suggest something more hopeful in conversation with those worried about global backsliding and offered from the perspective and behavior of the voters we study.

First, whether measured on surveys or directly observed, citizens in emerging democracies articulate demands and participate in competitive elections by healthy margins. Robust turnout may be curious, but it is also vital – yet there is no moment when institutions in any country are suddenly perfectly consolidated. Democratic progress requires not only a transition to well-administered elections but also the persistent vigilance to maintain institutions by the body politic. In moments of uncertainty or peril, this suggests a reaffirmation of normative commitments to democracy and encouragement to participate rather than abandonment or disengagement. The fact that turnout remains high – decades after transition and even during a global pandemic – is proof of citizens' ongoing investment in democracy.

Second, voters in developing countries use access to formal institutions they have gained since transition in ways to improve life around them. Rather than stay home and free-ride, they are leveraging the advantages their social and electoral environments provide them to enhance the availability and quality of services in their communities. Despite democratic imperfections, life for the average citizen – measured by income, educational attainment, or health – is often better today than life under dictatorship. This has been true in many third-wave countries, including our African cases, even though their governments definitely have room to improve.

But what about Afghanistan, where democratization collapsed after 20 years of unprecedented investments in state-building and the construction of representative institutions? We suggest the lessons are not that different. Since the Taliban's victory, it has become fashionable to blame the failures of the civilian government on the United States, Ashraf Ghani personally, Pakistan, or to question whether democratization is ever possible in a fragile state or at least possible in Afghanistan. Less considered is the role of Afghan citizens in holding up or abandoning these institutions. That far fewer Afghans voted in the most recent elections compared to earlier years does not suggest they rejected democracy or welcomed the Taliban. Rather, as the government became increasingly incapable of providing services and otherwise actualizing democracy's benefits, the costs voters were willing to pay previously were eclipsed by a lack of government responsiveness. Afghans were no less strategic in their motivations for participation than Ghanaians and were no less strategic in 2019 than 2010; however, the bargain for participating had not taken root as it had in Ghana, and the prospects in 2019 were bleaker than 2010. Insofar as democracy first began to retreat in Afghanistan, it does not seem to have been at the behest of Afghan people, but rather the Afghan government (and subsequently the Taliban). As in our African cases, voters were doing their part.

We suspect that understanding global backsliding is therefore not so much a question of voters not taking elections seriously or participating for the "wrong" reasons. Voters continue to do the hard work to support democratic institutions, and citizens in communities have paid the high costs to embrace democracy, even seemingly overnight, if they have reasons to believe it matters. Instead, it seems the conversation should focus on how well institutions serve those voters. Considering these citizens' behavior against many and evolving obstacles, democracy in the twenty-first century may be less perilous than it often seems when accounting for the social origins of electoral participation.

References

Al-Jazeera. 2019. "Voter Turnout Falls Sharply in Afghan Presidential Election." November 29. www.aljazeera.com/news/2019/9/29/voter-turn out-falls-sharply-in-afghan-presidential-election.

Alizada, Nazifa, Rowan Cole, Lisa Gastaldi, et al. 2021. *Autocratization Turns Viral: Democracy Report 2021*.Gothenburg: University of Gothenburg, V-Dem Institute.

Ames, David W. 1959. "Wolof Co-operative Work Groups." In *Continuity and Change in African Cultures*, ed. William Bascom and Melville J. Herskovitz. Chicago: University of Chicago Press.

Asia Foundation. 2019. *A Survey of the Afghan People: Afghanistan in 2019.* San Francisco: The Asia Foundation.

Atkinson, Matthew D., and Anthony Fowler. 2014. "Social Capital and Voter Turnout." *British Journal of Political Science* 44(1): 41–59.

Baldwin, Kate. 2016. *The Paradox of Traditional Chiefs in Democratic Africa.* Cambridge: Cambridge University Press.

Banerjee, Mukulika. 2007. "Sacred Elections." *Economic and Political Weekly* 42(17): 1556–62.

Barfield, Thomas. 2010. *Afghanistan*. Princeton: Princeton University Press.

Barkan, Joel. 1997. "African Elections in Comparative Perspective." In *Elections: Perspectives on Establishing Democratic Practices*, ed. United Nations Department for Development Support and Management Services. New York: United Nations Department for Development Support and Management Services, 3–27. https://digitallibrary.un.org/record/247744/files/ST_TCD_SER.E_31-EN.pdf.

Bauer, Michal, Christopher Blattman, Julie Chytilová, et al. 2016. "Can War Foster Cooperation?" *Journal of Economic Perspectives* 30(3): 249–74.

BBC. 2008. "Tsvangirai Rejects 'Sham' Ballot." June 27. http://news.bbc.co.uk/2/hi/africa/7478399.stm.

Beaulieu, Emily. 2014. *Electoral Protest and Democracy in the Developing World*. Cambridge: Cambridge University Press.

Bekoe, Dorina A., and Stephanie M. Burchard. 2017. "The Contradictions of Pre-election Violence." *African Studies Review* 60(2): 73–92.

Berman, Eli, Michael Callen, Clark Gibson, James D. Long and Arman Rezaee. 2019. "Election Fairness and Government Legitimacy in Afghanistan." *Journal of Economic Behavior & Organization* 168: 292–317.

Blattman, Christopher, Mathilde Emeriau, and Nathan Fiala. 2018. "Do Anti-Poverty Programs Sway Voters?" *The Review of Economics and Statistics* 100(5): 891–905.

Blattman, Christopher, Horacio Larreguy, Benjamin Marx, and Otis R. Reid. 2019. "Eat Widely, Vote Wisely?" National Bureau of Economic Research Working Paper. www.nber.org/papers/w26293.

Boulding, Carew, and Claudio Holzner. 2021. *Voice and Inequality.* Oxford: Oxford University Press.

Bratton, Michael, Robert Mattes, and E. Gyimah-Boadi. 2005. *Public Opinion, Democracy, and Market Reform in Africa.* Cambridge: Cambridge University Press.

Bukenya, Badru, and Sam Hickey. 2019. "The Shifting Fortunes of the Economic Technocracy in Uganda: Caught between State-Building and Regime Survival?" Pockets of Effectiveness Working Paper No 5. June 17. Manchester: University of Manchester. https://ssrn.com/abstract=3467495 or http://dx.doi.org/10.2139/ssrn.3467495.

Burbidge, Dominic. 2014. "'Can Someone Get Me Outta This Middle Class Zone?!'" *The Journal of Modern African Studies* 52(2): 205–25.

Byarugaba, Foster. 2003. "Bunyoro Voters Wary of 'Unholy' Alliances in 1996 Elections." In *Voting for Democracy in Uganda,* ed. Sabiti Makara, Geoffrey B. Tukahebwa, and Foster Byarugaba. Kampala: LDC Publishers, 90–115.

Callen, Michael, Clark Gibson, Danielle F. Jung, and James D. Long. 2016. "Improving Electoral Integrity with Information and Communications Technology." *Journal of Experimental Political Science* 3(1): 4–17.

Chandra, Kanchan. 2004. *Why Ethnic Parties Succeed.* Cambridge: Cambridge University Press.

Cheeseman, Nic, Gabrielle Lynch, and Justin Willis. 2021. *The Moral Economy of Elections in Africa.* Cambridge: Cambridge University Press.

Coburn, Noah. 2016. *Losing Afghanistan.* Stanford: Stanford University Press.

Coburn, Noah, and Anna Larson. 2014. *Derailing Democracy in Afghanistan.* New York: Columbia University Press.

Condra, Luke N., Michael Callen, Radha Iyengar, James D. Long, and Jacob Shapiro. 2019. "Damaging Democracy? Security Provision and Turnout in Afghan Elections." *Economics & Politics* 31(2): 163–93.

Condra, Luke N., James D. Long, Andrew C. Shaver, and Austin L. Wright. 2018. "The Logic of Insurgent Electoral Violence." *American Economic Review* 108(11): 3199–231.

Darnolf, Staffan, Fernanda Buril, and Meredith Applegate. 2020. "Indelible Ink in Elections: Mitigating Risks of COVID-19 Transmission While

Maintaining Effectiveness." International Foundation for Electoral Systems. April 15. www.ifes.org/news/indelible-ink-elections-mitigating-risks-covid-19-transmission-while-maintaining-effectiveness.

Dickson, Eric S., and Kenneth Scheve. 2006. "Social Identity, Political Speech, and Electoral Competition." *Journal of Theoretical Politics* 18(1): 5–39.

Dobler, Gregor. 2019. "Waiting and Voting in the Village: Election Day 2014 in Odibo, Namibia." *Journal of Namibian Studies* 26: 7–28.

Downs, Anthony. 1957. *An Economic Theory of Democracy.* New York: Harper & Row.

Dreier, Sarah K., James D. Long, and Stephen Winkler. 2020. "African, Religious, and Tolerant?" *Politics and Religion* 13(2): 273–303.

Dupuy, Beatrice. 2017. "Kenyan Women Hold Election Sex Strike to Get Their Husbands to Vote Their Candidate." *Newsweek.* October 23. www.news week.com/women-hold-sex-strike-kenyan-election-690648.

The Economist. 2022. "Afghans Are More Pessimistic about Their Future Than Ever." January 29. www.economist.com/asia/2022/01/29/afghans-are-more-pessimistic-about-their-future-than-ever.

Economist Intelligence Unit. 2021. *Democracy Index 2020: In Sickness and in Health?* London: The Economist. www.eiu.com/n/campaigns/democracy-index-2020/.

Erlich, Aaron. 2020. "Can Information Campaigns Impact Preferences toward Vote Selling?" *International Political Science Review* 41(3): 419–35.

Fafchamps, Marcel. 2003. *Market Institutions in Sub-Saharan Africa: Theory and Evidence.* Cambridge, MA: MIT Press.

Ferree, Karen E., Clark Gibson, and James D. Long. 2014. "Voting Behavior and Electoral Irregularities in Kenya's 2013 Election." *Journal of Eastern African Studies* 8(1): 153–72.

    2021. "Mixed Records, Complexity, and Ethnic Voting in African Elections." *World Development* 141: 105418.

Ferree, Karen E., Danielle F. Jung, Robert A. Dowd, and Clark Gibson. 2020. "Election Ink and Turnout in a Partial Democracy." *British Journal of Political Science* 50(3): 1175–91.

Ferree, Karen E., and James D. Long. 2016. "Gifts, Threats, and Perceptions of Ballot Secrecy in African Elections." *African Affairs* 115(461): 621–45.

Finan, Frederico, and Laura Schechter. 2012. "Vote-Buying and Reciprocity." *Econometrica* 80(2): 863–81.

France 24. 2017. "Polling Stations Open in Kenya despite Calls for Boycott." www.france24.com/en/20171026-polling-booths-open-kenya-despite-calls-boycott-vote.

Franklin, Mark N. 2004. *Voter Turnout and the Dynamics of Electoral Competition in Established Democracies since 1945*. Cambridge: Cambridge University Press.

Gachuhi, Kennedy. 2017. "Bars to Remain Closed on Elections Day." *The Standard*. www.standardmedia.co.ke/rift-valley/article/2001250410/bars-to-remain-closed-on-elections-day.

Gerber, Alan, Donald P. Green, and Christopher W. Larimer. 2008. "Social Pressure and Voter Turnout." *American Political Science Review* 102(01): 33–48.

Gibson, Clark, and James D. Long. 2009. "The Presidential and Parliamentary Elections in Kenya, December 2007." *Electoral Studies* 28(3): 497–502.

Gingyera-Pinyewa, A. G. G., and Quintas Obong-Oula. 2003. "The Political 'Moods' of Northern Uganda, 1986-96: A Study of the Presidential and Parliamentary Elections." In *Voting for Democracy in Uganda*, ed. S. Makara, G. Tukahebwa, and F. Byarugaba. Kampala: LDC Publishers, 55–89.

Githongo, John. 2007. "Kenya's Fight against Corruption." Cato Institute Development Briefing Paper. www.cato.org/development-briefing-paper/kenyas-fight-against-corruption-uneven-path-political-accountability.

Golooba-Mutebi, Frederick, and Sam Hickey. 2016. "The Master of Institutional Multiplicity?" *Journal of Eastern African Studies* 10: 601–18.

Gopal, Anand. 2014. *No Good Men among the Living*. New York: Metropolitan Books.

Gottlieb, Jessica, and Horacio Larreguy. 2020. "An Informational Theory of Electoral Targeting in Young Clientelistic Democracies." *Quarterly Journal of Political Science* 15(1): 73–104.

Graphic Online. 2020. "Dumelo Wants Voting Halted at Polling Station over the Absence of Indelible Ink." www.graphic.com.gh/news/politics/dumelo-wants-voting-halted-at-polling-station-over-the-absence-of-indelible-ink.html.

Greif, Avner. 1993. "Contract Enforceability and Economic Institutions in Early Trade." *American Economic Review* 83(3): 525–48.

Guardado, Jennifer, and Leonard Wantchekon. 2018. "Do Electoral Handouts Affect Voting Behavior?" *Electoral Studies* 53 (June): 139–49.

Haggard, Stephan, and Robert Kaufman. 2021. "Backsliding: Democratic Regress in the Contemporary World." *Elements in Political Economy*. Cambridge: Cambridge University Press.

Harding, Robin. 2015. "Attribution and Accountability." *World Politics* 67(4): 656–89.

Harris, J. Andrew. 2021. "Election Administration, Resource Allocation, and Turnout." *Comparative Political Studies* 54(3–4): 623–51.

Harris, J. Andrew, and Daniel Posner. 2019. "(Under What Conditions) Do Politicians Reward Their Supporters?" *American Political Science Review* 113(1): 123–39.

Hoffman, Barak, and James D. Long. 2013. "Parties, Ethnicity, and Voting in African Elections." *Comparative Politics* 45: 127–46.

Horowitz, Donald. 1985. *Ethnic Groups in Conflict.* Berkeley: University of California.

Horowitz, Jeremy, and James D. Long. 2016. "Strategic Voting, Information, and Ethnicity in Emerging Democracies: Evidence from Kenya." *Electoral Studies* 44(December): 351–61.

Huntington, Samuel. 1993. *The Third Wave.* Norman: University of Oklahoma.

Ichino, Nahomi, and Noah Nathan. 2013. "Crossing the Line" *American Political Science Review* 107(2): 344–61.

  2022. "Democratizing the Party." *British Journal of Political Science* 52(3): 1–18.

IDEA. 2021. "Voter Turnout Database." International Idea. www.idea.int/data-tools/country-view/156/40.

Jung, Danielle F. 2012. "Organizational Ecology and Population Dynamics in Politics: An Agent-Based Model." Doctoral dissertaion, University of California, San Diego.

Jung, Danielle F., and Dara Kay Cohen. 2020. *Lynching and Local Justice.* Cambridge: Cambridge University Press.

Jung, Danielle F., and David A. Lake. 2011a. "Markets, Hierarchies, and Networks." *American Journal of Political Science* 55(4): 972–90.

  2011b. "Organizations and the Evolution of Cooperation." Political Networks Conference Paper 5. http://opensiuc.lib.siu.edu/pnconfs_2011/5.

Kah, Jainaba, Dana Olds, and Muhammadou Kah. 2005. "Microcredit, Social Capital, and Politics: The Case of a Small Rural Town – Gossas, Senegal." *Journal of Microfinance/ESR Review* 7(1): 121–52.

Kakumba, Makanga Ronald. 2020. "Double Standard? Ugandans See Vote Buying as 'Wrong and Punishable,' Vote Selling Less So." www.afroba rometer.org/publication/ad415-double-standard-ugandans-see-vote-buy ing-wrong-and-punishable-vote-selling-less/.

Kanyinga, Karuti, James D. Long, and David Ndii. 2010. "Was It Rigged?" In *Tensions and Reversals in Democratic Transitions*, ed. Karuti Kanyinga and Duncan Okello. Nairobi: University of Nairobi Press, 373–414.

Kasara, Kimuli, and Pavithra Suryanarayan. 2015. "When Do the Rich Vote Less Than the Poor and Why?" *American Journal of Political Science* 59(3): 613–27.

Khalilzad, Zalmay. 2016. *The Envoy*. New York: St. Martin's Press.

Kitschelt, Herbert, and Steven I. Wilkinson. 2007. *Patrons, Clients and Policies*. Cambridge: Cambridge University Press.

Klaus, Kathleen, and Jeffrey W. Paller. 2017. "Defending the City, Defending Votes." *The Journal of Modern African Studies* 55(4): 681–708.

Kokutse, Francis. 2020. "Ghana Votes for President in Test of Country's Stability." *Associated Press*. December 7. https://apnews.com/article/ ghana-coronavirus-pandemic-elections-africa-john-dramani-mahama-1aebbd51adf3a42f92417f8ff33b624e.

Kostelka, Filip. 2017. "Does Democratic Consolidation Lead to a Decline in Voter Turnout?" *American Political Science Review* 111(4): 653–67.

Kraemer, Richard. 2014. "Can Afghanistan Survive Its Presidential Election?" Foreign Policy Research Institute. August 29. www.fpri.org/article/2014/ 08/can-afghanistan-survive-its-presidential-election/.

Kramon, Eric. 2016. "Where Is Vote Buying Effective?" *Electoral Studies* 44: 397–408.

Kuenzi, Michelle, and Gina M. S. Lambright. 2007. "Voter Turnout in Africa's Multiparty Regimes." *Comparative Political Studies* 40(6): 665–90.

2011. "Who Votes in Africa?" *Party Politics* 17(6): 767–99.

Larvie, John. 2008. "Oral History Program Series: Elections." https://success fulsocieties.princeton.edu/sites/successfulsocieties/files/interviews/tran scripts/3230/John_Larvie.txt.

Levitsky, Steven, and Lucan Way. 2010. *Competitive Authoritarianism*. Cambridge: Cambridge University Press.

Long, James. D. 2012. "Voting, Fraud, and Violence." Doctoral dissertation, University of California, San Diego.

2020. "Civil Conflict, Power Sharing, Truth and Reconciliation (2005–2013)." In *Oxford Handbook of Kenyan Politics*, ed. Nic Cheeseman, Karuti Kanyinga, and Gabrielle Lynch. Oxford: Oxford University Press, 82–95.

Long, James D., and Clark Gibson. 2015. "Evaluating the Roles of Ethnicity and Performance in African Elections." *Political Research Quarterly* 68 (4): 830–42.

Long, James D., Karuti Kanyinga, Karen E. Ferree, and Clark Gibson. 2013. "Kenya's 2013 Elections." *Journal of Democracy* 24(3): 140–55.

Lynge-Mangueira, Halfdan. 2013. "How to Rig an Election and What Two Constituencies in Ghana Might Teach Us about Defining and Measuring

Electoral Rigging." Presented at the Electoral Integrity Project Annual Workshop, Weatherhead Center, Harvard University, Cambridge, MA.

Magdy, Samy. 2019. "Rights Group Denounces 'Unfree and Unfair' Egyptian Vote." *Associated Press*. April 24. https://apnews.com/article/ea048eec 24a0417ca0255e1e559a709c.

Makara, Sabiti. 2003a. "Voting for Democracy in Uganda" In *Voting for Democracy in Uganda*, ed. Sabiti Makara, Geoffrey B. Tukahebwa, and Foster Byarugaba. Kampala: LDC Publishers, 1–32.

　　2003b. "The Buganda Issues in Electoral Politics during the 1996 Presidential Elections." In *Voting for Democracy in Uganda*, ed. Sabiti Makara, Geoffrey B. Tukahebwa, and Foster Byarugaba. Kampala: LDC Publishers, 116–35.

Mares, Isabela, and Lauren Young. 2016. "Buying, Expropriating, and Stealing Votes." *Annual Review of Political Science* 19(1): 267–88.

Mari, Gloria. 2019. "Confessions of a Jubilee Supporter." *The Elephant*. April 24. www.theelephant.info/reflections/2019/05/24/confessions-of-a-jubilee-supporter/

Mitullah, Winnie V. 2015. "Negotiated Democracy." In *Kenya's 2013 General Election*, ed. Kimani Kjogu and Peter Wafula Wekesa. Nairobi: Twaweza Communications.

Mpagi, Charles. 2018. "Return of Queue Voting System in Uganda." *The East African*. July 4. www.theeastafrican.co.ke/tea/news/east-africa/return-of-queue-voting-system-in-uganda-1397500.

Murtazashvili, Jennifer. 2016. *Informal Order and the State in Afghanistan*. Cambridge: Cambridge University Press.

Musambi, Evelyne. 2017. "Electoral Commission Wins Rare Praise from Kenyans." *Nairobi News*. August 8. https://nairobinews.nation.co.ke/news/electoral-commission-wins-praise-kenyans.

Nathan, Noah L. 2019a. "Electoral Consequences of Colonial Invention." *World Politics* 71(3): 417–56.

　　2019b. *Electoral Politics and Africa's Urban Transition*. Cambridge: Cambridge University Press.

Ndiso, John. 2017. "Some Kenyans, Keen to Vote, Rent Babies to Jump Long Queues." *Reuters*. August 8. www.reuters.com/article/us-kenya-election-babies-idUSKBN1AO1J1.

Nichter, Simeon. 2008. "Vote Buying or Turnout Buying?" *American Political Science Review* 102(1): 19–31.

　　2018. *Votes for Survival*. Cambridge: Cambridge University Press.

Nugent, Paul. 2006. "Banknotes and Symbolic Capital" In *Votes, Money and Violence*, ed. A Mehler. Uppsala: Nordic Africa Institute.

Odote, Collins. 2020. "The 2013 Elections and the Peace Narrative (2013–2015)." In *Oxford Handbook of Kenyan Politics*, ed. Nic Cheeseman, Karuti Kanyinga, and Gabrielle Lynch. Oxford: Oxford University Press, 96–108.

Oloo, Adams. 2020. "The Weaknesses of Political Parties." In *Oxford Handbook of Kenyan Politics*, ed. Nic Cheeseman, Karuti Kanyinga, and Gabrielle Lynch. Oxford: Oxford University Press.

Olson, Mancur. 1965. *The Logic of Collective Action*. Cambridge, MA: Harvard University Press.

Osborn, Michelle. 2020. "Chiefs, Elders, and Traditional Authority." In *Oxford Handbook of Kenyan Politics*, ed. Nic Cheeseman, Karuti Kanyinga, and Gabrielle Lynch. Oxford: Oxford University Press, 297–309.

Ostrom, Elinor. 1990 *Governing the Commons*. Cambridge: Cambridge University Press.

Paller, Jeffrey W. 2019. *Democracy in Ghana*. Cambridge: Cambridge University Press.

Parliament of Uganda. 2005. *Parliamentary Elections Act*. https://aceproject .org/ero-en/regions/africa/UG/uganda-parliamentary-elections-act–2005.

Partlow, Joshua. 2017. *A Kingdom of Their Own*. New York: Vintage Books.

Platteau, Jean-Philippe. 1991. "Traditional Systems of Social Security and Hunger Insurance: Past Achievements and Modern Challenges." In *Social Security in Developing Countries*, ed. Ehtisham Ahmad, Jean Dreze, John Hills, and Amartya K. Sen. Oxford: Clarendon Press, 112–70.

Popkin, Samuel, John Gorman, Charles Phillips, and Jeffrey Smith. 1976. "Comment: What Have You Done for Me Lately?" *American Political Science Review* 70(30): 779–805.

Repucci, Sarah, and Amy Slipowitz. 2021. *Freedom in the World 2021*. Washington, DC: Freedom House. https://freedomhouse.org/report/free dom-world/2021/democracy-under-siege.

Riker, William H., and Peter C. Ordeshook. 1968. "A Theory of the Calculus of Voting." *American Political Science Review* 62(1): 25–42.

Robinson, Amanda L. 2014. "National versus Ethnic Identification in Africa." *World Politics* 66(4): 709–46.

Rosenzweig, Leah R. 2019. "Social Voting in Semi-Authoritarian Systems." Working paper.

Schaffer, Frederic. 2003. *Democracy in Translation*. Ithaca, NY: Cornell University Press.

Stasavage, David. 2005. "The Role of Democracy in Uganda's Move to Universal Primary Education." *The Journal of Modern African Studies* 43(1): 53–73.

Scott, James. 1977. *The Moral Economy of the Peasant*. New Haven: Yale University Press.

Stokes, Susan, Thad Dunning, Marcelo Nazareno, and Valeria Brusco. 2013. *Brokers, Voters, and Clientelism*. Cambridge: Cambridge University Press.

Tapscott, Rebecca. 2016. "Where the Wild Things Are Not." *Journal of Eastern African Studies* 10(4): 693–712.

Tripp, Aili. 2010. *Museveni's Uganda*. Boulder: Lynne Rienner Publishers.

Human Rights Watch. 2021. "Uganda: Elections Marred by Violence." *Human Rights Watch*. June 27. www.hrw.org/news/2021/01/21/uganda-elections-marred-violence.

ULII. 2005. *Presidential Elections Act of 2005*. Part VI. https://ulii.org/akn/ug/act/2005/16/eng%402015-10-01.

Truth, Justice, and Reconciliation Commission of Kenya. 2008. *Commissions of Inquiry – CIPEV Report (Waki Report)*. Seattle: Seattle University School of Law Digital Commons. https://digitalcommons.law.seattleu.edu/tjrc-gov/5.

Uganda Electoral Commission. *Voter Education Messages on the Voting Process*. Kampala: Uganda Electoral Commission. www.ec.or.ug/pub/VE_messages.pdf.

VOA News. 2009. "Ghana Voters Combine Christmas With Political Gift-Giving." *VOA News*. October 27. https://www.voanews.com/a/a-13-2008-12-15-voa1-66737132/561740.html.

Wamai, Njoki. 2020. "International Relations and the International Criminal Court." In *Oxford Handbook of Kenyan Politics*, ed. Nic Cheeseman, Karuti Kanyinga, and Gabrielle Lynch. Oxford: Oxford University Press.

Wilder, Andrew. 2005. *A House Divided? Analysing the 2005 Afghan Elections*. Kabul: Afghanistan Research and Evaluation Unit. www.refworld.org/pdfid/47c3f3c01b.pdf.

Willis, Justin, Gabrielle Lynch, and Nic Cheeseman. 2017. "The Voting Machine: The Material Culture of Polling Stations in Ghana, Kenya, and Uganda." *Politique Africaine* 144(4): 27–50.

Young, Daniel J. 2009. "Is Clientelism at Work in African Elections?" Afrobarometer Working Paper No. 106. www.files.ethz.ch/isn/98869/AfropaperNo106.pdf.

About the Authors

Danielle F. Jung is Associate Professor of Political Science at Emory University. Her research focuses on understanding how political legitimacy is built and decays, particularly via service provision and governance by non-state organizations, as well as elections in fragile states.

James D. Long is Professor of Political Science and the co-founder of the Political Economy Forum at the University of Washington. His research focuses on democratization, elections, corruption, state-building, and the political economy of development.

Acknowledgments

This project was born over beers in Accra when we were graduate students and then sharpened via years-long discussions over more meals and wine, on the phone, Skype, Zoom, Whatsapp, looking at screens over each other's shoulder, and on too many white boards to count. We were also fortunate to share opportunities to observe elections over the next decade. As with any endeavor over such a long period, we have accrued countless debts. Many colleagues have shaped both this project and our scholarly trajectories to whom we owe much gratitude.

For comments and advice, we thank Joel Barkan (sadly no longer with us), Eli Berman, Eric Bjornlund, Mike Callen, Tom Clark, Luke Condra, Glenn Cowan, Karen Ferree, Jennifer Gandhi, Clark Gibson, Fred Golooba-Mutebi, Steph Haggard, Karuti Kanyinga, David Lake, Victor Menaldo, Craig McIntosh, Michael Leo Owens, Sam Popkin, Jake Shapiro, Branislav Slantchev, Jeff Staton, Venita Yadav, and seminar participants at Emory, Harvard, Princeton, UCSD, University of Washington, Institutions & Lawmaking Conference, and the Working Group in African Political Economy.

Our research would have been impossible without the dedicated work of numerous colleagues in Africa and Afghanistan, especially Kobina Graham, Nana Gyamenah, Maggie Ireri, Mohammad Isaqzadeh, Shahim Kabuli, Sara Kerosky, Hilda Kiritu, Kennedy Lukilah, Doreen Lwanga, Rachel Mukami, Samuel Muthoka, Marie Nanyanzi, Virginia Nkwanzi, Arnold Nyakundi, Jed Ober, Lauren Pearson, and Philip Okullo.

Jintong Han, Anthony Luongo, Patrick Pierson, Morgan Wack, Adee Weller, and Stephen Winkler provided excellent research assistance.

When the pandemic hit and we could no longer travel to the field, Emily Beaulieu, Charles Stewart, and Mike Alvarez helped realize our vision into the Element format. Emily's guidance and those of two generous reviewers sharpened the frame we had been working toward for many years. We thank Ulrike Guthrie for excellent editorial assistance.

We received generous funding from the University of Washington, Harvard Academy for International & Area Studies, National Science Foundation, Empirical Studies of Conflict, Fulbright, Democracy International, Institute on Global Conflict & Cooperation, and the Emory Center for Teaching & Faculty Development.

We dedicate this book to our families, who offered constant love and support through missed holidays and shared celebrations, dropped phone calls, and spotty internet to allow us the privilege to experience the momentous (and yes, frequently nerve-wracking) elections this project required. We also give special thanks to the thousands of Ghanaians, Kenyans, Ugandans, and Afghans who graciously lent their time to answer our surveys. Although democracy is far from perfect in these countries – and has collapsed tragically in Afghanistan – we stand in awe of their citizens as they work to improve electoral institutions, government accountability, and the lives of those in their communities and countries. We are especially lucky to consider what they have taught us about democracy in our own country – where voting is easier, although persistently under threat and all too often taken for granted.

Cambridge Elements ≡

Campaigns and Elections

R. Michael Alvarez
California Institute of Technology

R. Michael Alvarez is Professor of Political and Computational Social Science at Caltech. His current research focuses on election administration and technology, campaigns and elections, and computational modeling.

Emily Beaulieu Bacchus
University of Kentucky

Emily Beaulieu Bacchus is Associate Professor of Political Science and Director of International Studies at the University of Kentucky. She is an expert in political institutions and contentious politics – focusing much of her work on perceptions of election fraud and electoral protests. Electoral Protest and Democracy in the Developing World was published with Cambridge University Press in 2014.

Charles Stewart III
Massachusetts Institute of Technology

Charles Stewart III is the Kenan Sahin Distinguished Professor of Political Science at MIT. His research and teaching focus on American politics, election administration, and legislative politics.

About the Series

Broadly focused, covering electoral campaigns & strategies, voting behavior, and electoral institutions, this Elements series offers the opportunity to publish work from new and emerging fields, especially those at the interface of technology, elections, and global electoral trends.

Cambridge Elements ≡

Campaigns and Elections